Louis des Cognets Jr.

Radnor, Pa.

19 22/IX 55

MEMOIR

OF

CHARLOTTE CHAMBERS.

By her Grandson,

LEWIS H. GARRARD.

PHILADELPHIA:
PRINTED FOR THE AUTHOR.
1856.

PRINTED BY T. K. AND P. G. COLLINS.

To Mrs. Sarah Bella M'Lean.

My Dear Mother:

I wish to inscribe this book to you.

When in the past summer, you placed in my hands the letters which had been treasured by you these past thirty years with all the devotion of a daughter's affection, I felt that the trust was far greater than my capability to fulfil. You well know that I approached the task with much diffidence; for I was sensible of a want of that Christian spirit, and that refinement of appreciation, necessary to the preparation of a memoir of so sacred a character as this.

From you I early learned to revere the subject of this memoir. And while now away from your presence, as I read the precious letters which your hand—long ere mine knew how to trace them—transcribed from the faded and dismembered originals, your image is ever before me. Could a son desire a more touching duty than the compilation of these letters thus hallowed by a mother's care, or wish the hours of contemplative seclusion more acceptably employed?

But whatever the merit of preserving the sentiments in this book—whatever of filial love and respect their committal to print will show, must be accorded to you, and to you alone—I have been but the instrument to execute your design.

LEWIS.

PREFACE.

In reviewing a past era, we usually accept in the absence of other evidence, the characteristics of its prominent actors as the several personal types of that age; and whether those individuals have done vast evil, or accomplished much good, they surely stamp its reputation.

But turning from this high-road of humanity's journeying into the unobtrusive paths trod by the simply devout and exemplary, we see that their lives—though replete with deeds pleasing in the sight of Heaven and illustrating the virtues of a community contributing largely to the general public morals—lack the brilliancy and the salient points which fascinate and retain the attention after death has resolved into dust all that was mortal, and forever stilled the voice that was not heard, save in the cause of love, justice, and mercy.

Often, however, there are recollections too vivid, and written indications of traits too decided, to permit the dulling influence of time, with its obliterating tide of a new and careless generation, to bear its wonted sway. Occasionally also, these are dear to some reverential member of the family, who would thus enshrine the excellencies of the departed by placing in permanent and convenient form, those thoughts that win the way to our kindly sympathies with their gentle euphony, and increase our esteem of the one who penned them, by their elevating tendency and strongly pervading sense of the Christian graces.

It is much to be regretted that the lapse of many years has prevented the reclamation of but a fragmentary portion of the letters of Charlotte Chambers; and sadder yet to say, that even of these a large number were irrecoverably mislaid. Still, it is trusted, that the few here presented will be welcomed as a slight tribute to the debt long since due—and if their perusal will impart the natural gratification of witnessing a clear record of those who have "gone before," and aid in cherishing in the minds of descendants the laudable desire of continuing the name and lineage in the course of probity and respectability, the writer will truly feel that his earnest purpose has not been entirely without some value.

HISTORICAL SKETCH.

NOTE.

The principal works consulted for this Sketch are the Colonial Records and Archives of Pennsylvania; Gordon's History of Pennsylvania; Rupp's History of Cumberland and other Counties; the files of the Pennsylvania Gazette from 1745 to 1762 inclusive; Colonel Nicola's MS. list of Officers of the Revolution; the Order Books of Colonel James Chambers, from July 26th, 1778, to August 5th, 1780; and Rev. Alfred Nevin's work, entitled Churches in the Valley.

To these—to the friendly attentions of Judge George Chambers and Mr. Thomas Chambers—to the library of the Historical Society, and the kindness of his fellow-members of the Society, Mr. Samuel Hazard, Mr. John Jordan, Jr., Mr. Henry C. Baird, and, in an especial and grateful manner, to Mr. Townsend Ward, the writer is indebted for aid in dispelling the mists which have accumulated around the subjects herein treated of in the past one hundred and thirty years.

HISTORICAL SKETCH.

THE COLONY.

ABOUT the year seventeen hundred and twenty-six, four brothers—of Scotch descent, residents of County Antrim, Ireland—allured by the bright prospects of fortune in the New World, forsook the comforts of a pleasant home and the familiar scenery of the picturesque LOUGH NEAGH, and wended their way to the distant province of Pennsylvania.

Of these, Benjamin Chambers was the youngest, who thus, at the early age of seventeen, had chosen the arduous and attractive life of a pioneer.[1]

[1] The first mention of the name of Chambers in the province is in the following transaction from the Pennsylvania Archives, vol. i. p. 39. One of the persons named was probably the father of the four brothers:—

"To my Loving Fr^d THOMAS HOLMS, Surveyor-General of Pennsylvania, greeting:—

"These are to Authorize thee to Set out ye Survey'd Bounds to the Respective purchasers use, according to the last Lists of Purchasers Sent by Philip Ford, and by him Signed according to Authority. Given him by me, and for so doing this shall be thy Sufficient Warrant. Given under my hand this 22^d day of 3 m^o 1682.

"WM. PENN [L. S.] ℘ PHILIP FORD.

"An Account of the Lands in Pennsylvania granted by William Penn,

With ample means at their control, and predilections in favor of no particular section, the brothers, after their arrival in Philadelphia, took sufficient leisure to gain information of the choicest portions of the back country.

Hearing much in praise of the rich soil and good timber of what was then the remote Susquehanna, they proceeded thither, and, near the mouth of Fishing Creek,[1] put up a mill, and appropriated a tract of excellent land.

The beautiful Cumberland Valley, or, as it was termed in the poetic language of the Indian, the Kittatinny,[2] or "endless," hemmed in by parallel ranges of pine-clad hills, stretched from beyond the Delaware River in New Jersey, across Pennsylvania and through Virginia to North Carolina.

In this valley, west of the Susquehanna to the temporary line dividing the provinces of Pennsylvania and Maryland, on the margins of the streams, the rudely shaped wigwams of the Lenni Lenape were placed.

Open patches of prairie, undulating enough for certain

Esq., Chief Proprietary and Governour of that Province, to Several Purchasers within the Kingdom of England, Ireland, and Scotland, &c.

		Acres.
"List No. 30.	Benjamin Chambers	1,000.
	"John Chambers	,500."

[1] Now in Dauphin County. Namáeshanne is the Lenni Lenape term for Fish Creek.

[2] In a deed by "The Five Nations Inhabiting in the Province of New York," for lands on Susquehanna to John, Thomas, and Richard Penn, these "are called, in the language of the said Nations, the Tyannuntasacta, or the Endless hills ; and, by the Delaware Indians, the *Kekkachtananin.*"—*Pa. Archives*, vol. i. p. 494.

drainage, and cleared of timber so long before the furthest reaching memory as to be traditional, invited easy culture for the corn and beans and pumpkin; the marshy spots afforded the red willow, or "kinniconick," for pleasing admixture with the soothing and precious tobacco; and the thickets hard by, no small variety of indigenous refreshing fruits. In the contiguous lordly parks, herds of timid deer and stalking bands of elk, unmolested except for the demands of hunger and limited trade, fattened on the nutritious grasses of the summer and browsed the swelling tree buds of the snowy season; while the limpid brooks yielded their treasures of beaver and otter and lusty-sided trout.

The white man, venturing in this primeval seclusion, often in his wanderings, directed by the sound of merry voices, would stumble on troops of nimble-footed girls swinging on the elastic green boughs or wading the brook, and making the old woods reëcho with the excess of unrestrained glee; while not far off, knots of bare-legged embryonic young warriors were taking first lessons in archery by stealthy, persevering, and murderous attempts on wrens and scolding catbirds.

But the strange sight of a pale face would act like magic in producing a silence as profound as the laughter a moment before was extravagant. Some would stand still in frightened indecision. Others would hurriedly seek the protecting skirts of the dark-eyed squaws, who, with the exclamatory "tiyah!" of surprise, would announce the arrival to the host within, by whom the stranger was welcomed to the most honored seat in the humble lodge.

Soon the assiduous care of the women would produce a wooden bowl of savory venison or steaming "suck-a-tash," to which his regards would be paid in a manner complimentary either to the skill of the admiring cooks or his own gastronomic ability.

That finished, the post-prandial pipe of amity was whiffed with becoming gravity by him and his host; and, when the news were deliberately and monosyllabically discussed, and the shades of night had descended, the grateful pallet of dried leaves and overlying skins sustained his tired limbs in invigorating quiescence.

The equitable and Christian policy of Penn's government taught the Indian to respect the English. Disarmed of suspicion, he became confiding. In the impulse of a simple heart, and with a sincere wish to serve his visitor, he pointed out the arable lands, the best fishing and hunting grounds, and in unaffected generosity invited him to partake freely, and without price, of the many advantages of the happy valley.

All this region to the west of the Susquehanna was not then offered for sale (nor even purchased of the aborigines until 1736), but the proprietaries of the Royal Grant, with the consent of the tribes, encouraged settlement therein. This was in pursuance of a liberal system, as well as to prevent the encroachments of the Maryland colony, whose frontier posts were creeping westward, but too much in a northern direction to suit the views of the Pennsylvania grantees.

In the excursions of the Lenapes to the mills of the Chambers', their rich peltries and uniformly favorable accounts of the country whence they came, excited the desire of Benjamin and Joseph to see it. A love of exploration and adventure, with perhaps an approximate similarity in the features of this newer Canaan to the hills and glens of their boyhood's rovings, led them to various parts of it, until directed by a hunter's glowing description of the superior water-power at the junction of the Falling Spring with the Conococheague,[1] they there rested in the assurance of having realized their expectations.

The former stream commenced in the confluence of several large springs, and held its meandering way through natural meadows, sometimes half hid by tussocks of long grass, sometimes overarched by impenetrable copses of the thorny plum, that bent to the weight of its golden drupes and the matted interlacing of purple-clustered vines. Then it collected in deep glassy pools, where the speckled trout sported in the bright sunshine, and darted away on the slightest sound of crackling brush or incautious voice to the safe refuge of a submerged log, or the intricacies of friendly tree-roots laid bare by the washing of the current; then it rushed with musical murmur in glittering miniature cascades, and over loose stones in the shallow channel, and through mossy banks garlanded with pale wild flowers, and hung with dripping aquatic plants, and again spread out in broad placid sheets, which reflected in the stillness of the glimmering noontide the wide leaves and branchless stems

[1] This was called by the Indians Guneukisschik, meaning "Indeed a long way. The word appears to refer to some cause where they became impatient."—*Heckewelder*.

of huge sycamores, standing on the water's edge—where scary schools of minnows rejoiced secure from the rapacious maws of the larger fish, and the summer fly lazily buzzed through its eccentric gyrations, an easy prey to the swift-winged swallow that, with eager eye and voluble twitter, lightly skimmed the air. Finally, the brook contracted for the impetuous leap from rock to rock, and in foam, and mist, and rapid rill mingled with the waters of the Conococheague.

Benjamin at once took possession of the most valuable portion of this locality. His first improvement, which constituted the foundation of Chambersburg in 1730, was a log house; and, what was unusual at that day, the timbers composing it were hewn, and it was roofed with lapped cedar shingles, fastened with nails. This was burned during his absence to the Susquehanna for supplies by some unprincipled person, whose cupidity was aroused for the sake of the iron used in its construction.

In an advantageous position, a saw-mill, and subsequently, a grist-mill, were erected. Other buildings were arranged in convenient order. Near by, in a cedar grove, was the dwelling separated from the mill by the race, which was crossed on a rustic wooden bridge.

In the course of a few years, the fertile meadows near were inclosed, and gave good return to the seed planted therein. With care and judgment, the cattle multiplied and improved in quality; horses roamed about half wild; goats nipped the tender herbage between the rocks; and geese and ducks, diving among the water-weeds, or floating majestically with the stream, added grace to the scene, and caused irresistible and cheering references to the calendar of feast days. In the garden, the rarest fruits and flowers of that time flourished; and the orchard (of which a few trees are now standing) was famous far and near.

The utility of the mills, and the kind disposition and religious faith of Mr. Chambers, were highly instrumental in settling the adjacent country. The people at Falling Spring were almost exclusively Scotch Irish Presbyterians. These brought with them from their native land, and rigidly maintained, the strict discipline of the Scottish creed, which calls the first day of the week the Sabbath—which demanded on that day, complete banishment from the mind of aught else than communion with holy things.

The Sabbath there was in striking contrast with the rest of the week. It was a period of delicious repose, in which surrounding nature seemed to participate. The sun beamed with genial lustre, performed its course, and gently waned beyond the hills, as if in accordance with the character of the day. The shrill note of the cock pierced the bracing morning air, and the impatient neighing of the horses shut up in the barn was more plainly heard than at other times. The lowing of the cows, anxious to be freed from the security of the night-inclosure, was modulated to a low, grateful moan as they slowly emerged, one by one, over the half-let-down bars to pull the fresh grass, yet sparkling with moistening dews. The water-fowl sailed noiselessly under the fringing alders of the mill-pond, or basked motionless in its centre; and the tinkling of the cataract, now that the stream was diverted from the silent water-wheel, struck softly in delicate, crystal notes on the delighted ear.

In the house, the harmony was complete with the occasion. In deferential respect, the men were smoothly shaved, and clad in coarse, but cleanly garb. The children presented a bright array of decent clothes, polished, ruddy faces, and recently combed hair; while the good wife, ever present and ever kind, neat and skilful, prepared the moderate morning meal, which was despatched with becoming sobriety. When the table was cleared, the cloth folded, and order restored, the old russet-bound Family Bible, which had been their constant companion over land and over sea from the home of their youth, was taken from its shelf, and laid near the man who read aloud the blessed words of inspiration. Then, on bended knee, with his little flock clustered around him, he lifted his voice in supplication to the Almighty Ruler to accept the joint peace-offering of penitent hearts.

No fire, save for the merest necessities, was kindled on the kitchen-hearth; nor was the day by questionable conventional license, scandalized by being converted into a period of feasting and sacrilegious hilarity. The Bible was read earnestly and intelligently; and the retentive memories of these settlers of Conococheague, made its history and its precepts, as illustrated by the Confession of Faith, household words. The children, reared without the adventitious aid of fine churches and bells, and other helps to Godliness in the cities, regarded the Sabbath at first with mysterious awe, until increase of age, and corresponding reason, assisted by the gradual inductions of the catechisms, explained its propriety, and taught them to follow the good example set by their devoted fathers and mothers.

Emigrating with prejudices intensified in favor of a faith that was born amidst tyranny and nurtured in fear and persecution--and cemented to the virtual exclusion of other sects in bonds of kindred sentiment for mutual protection and spiritual comfort in the depths of an inhospitable wilderness--their tenets may have lacked in charity, and their habits been too austere, and defence of their peculiar views on subjects involving principle, too vehement for those not of their blood, or own mode of thinking. They were harsh in accent, and perhaps rough in exterior, and they were not perfect in all things, for defects are human attributes; but beneath their manly breasts beat hearts teeming with firm resolve and high moral obligation.

MR. CHAMBERS had been at the Falling Springs for some years. He began to feel that the solitude so charming when wooed with the never-ending novelty of camp and travel, and the absorbing interest of a new settlement, was, in the comparative quiet of steady and concentrated employment, a wearying monotony. Family legend does not transmit a detail of the preliminary changes to this important step; but whatever may have been his youthful antipathies or maturer indifference, he succumbed at last, a willing sacrifice to natural law and generous affections. In

1741, he married the daughter of Captain Robert Patterson of Lancaster, who became the mother of his son James.

In 1748, several years subsequent to the death of his first wife, he was united to Miss Jane Williams, the daughter of an Episcopal clergyman of the Virginia colony from Wales. In the certificate of this marriage, he is styled colonel.[1] He also executed the duties of magistrate; and,

[1] "A masked and indirect war had been for some time carried on between France and Great Britain; and hostilities were openly declared by the former, on the 20th, and, by the latter, on the 31st of March (1744).

* * * * * *

"He (Gov. Thomas) commanded, by proclamation, all the able-bodied inhabitants to prepare arms, and commissioned officers, and appointed days for training.

* * * * * *

"The exertions of Franklin, on this occasion, contributed greatly to the security of the province, and to the preservation of harmony between the executive and the assembly. He published a pamphlet, entitled 'Plain Truth,' exhibiting, in strong lights, the helpless state of the province, and the necessity of union and discipline. Calling a meeting of the citizens, he laid before them a plan for a military association; twelve hundred signatures were immediately procured, and the volunteers soon amounted to ten thousand, armed at their own expense, and officered by their own choice. Franklin was chosen colonel of the Philadelphia regiment, but, declining the service, Alderman Lawrence was elected on his recommendation. By Franklin's means, also, a battery was erected below the city, from funds raised by lottery, in which Logan and many other Quakers, were adventurers. Logan, who was not scrupulous in relation to defensive war, directed whatever prizes he might draw, should be applied to the service of the battery.

"These military preparations were necessary to intimidate a foreign enemy, and to curb the hostile disposition of the Indians, which had

on account of his reputation for judgment and integrity, was, in his private capacity, frequently appealed to by his neighbors as arbiter of their difficulties. And, among other

been awakened by several unpleasant rencontres with the whites."—*Gordon's History of Pennsylvania*, pp. 244, 245.

The counties, in emulation of the noble example set by Philadelphia, furnished their quota of troops. Among the "officers chosen by the Associators, and commissioned by the Governor for that part of Lancaster County which lies between the river of Susquehannah and the Lines of the Province," are, for "Colonel, Benjamin Chambers, Esq.; Lieutenant-Colonel, Robert Dunning, Esq.; Major, William Maxwell, Esq."—*Pennsylvania Gazette*, March 22, 1748.

The following extracts are quite characteristic of the public temper and taste of the times:—

"Mottoes and Devices, painted on some of the Silk Colors of the Regiment of Associators in Philadelphia and country adjacent.

A Lion erect, a naked Scymeter in one Paw, the other holding the Pennsylvania Scutcheon. Motto: PRO PATRIA.

Three Arms wearing different Linnen ruffled, plain and chequed; the Hands joined by grasping each the other's Wrist, denoting the Union of all Ranks. Motto: UNITA VIRTUS VALET.

An Eagle, the Emblem of Victory, descending from the skies. Motto: A DEO VICTORIA.

The figure of LIBERTY sitting on a Cube, holding a Spear with the Cap of Freedom on its Point. Motto: INESTIMABILIS.

An Elephant, being the Emblem of a Warrior always on his Guard, as that Creature is said never to lie down, and hath his Arms ever in Readiness. Motto: SEMPER PARATUS.

A Coronet, and Plume of Feathers. Motto: IN GOD WE TRUST.

Three of the Associators, marching with their muskets shouldered, and dressed in different Clothes, intimating the Unanimity of the different Sorts of People in the Association. Motto: VIA UNITA FORTIOR.

Representation of a Glory, in the Middle of which is wrote, JEHOVAH NISSI; in English, The Lord our Banner.

duties of the head of a new colony, he performed the office of physician—gratuitously prescribing and administering medicine.

During the controversy between Lord Baltimore and the Penns, relative to the intermediate boundary of their respective provinces, which grew so bitter as to endanger the peace and prosperity of both, Mr. Chambers went to England, to assist, by his testimony, in determining the questions involved. So conclusive was his evidence in favor of the Penns, that they offered him any compensation he desired; and pressed his acceptance of a grant to a tract of land at the mouth of the Callapasscink,[1] the right to which was lost by neglect.

While absent on this mission, he visited his native soil, and induced many to accompany him on his return—he bearing the expenses of those unable to do so themselves.

The Indians of the vicinity of Falling Spring, viewed

David, as he advanced against Goliah and flung the Stone. Motto: IN NOMINE DOMINE.

The Duke of Cumberland as a General. Motto: PRO DEO AND GEORGIO REGE.

Most of the above colours, together with the Officers' Half-Pikes and Spontons, and even the Halberts, Drums, &c., have been given by the Good Ladies of this City, who raised money by Subscription, among themselves, for that Purpose."—*Pennsylvania Gazette*, January 12, and April 16, 1748.

[1] This is a Delaware Indian word, signifying a creek abounding in *horse-shoe* bends.—*Heckewelder*. For some reason now unknown, it was called the Yallerbritches Creek, which name, grammatically rendered and modernized, it still unfortunately bears.

with wonder, the useful customs and blameless life of the settlers. Ever treated with consideration, and receiving fair equivalent for articles of trade, they kept up friendly intercourse. Even after war was declared, neither the family nor the property of Mr. Chambers was molested by them. He spoke the language of the Delawares with facility, and was on familiar terms with them. Sometimes, however, in going to the fields to inspect his cattle, the large dogs accompanying him would denote by fierce barks, their presence, and the shaking of the bushes in the distance, mark their hasty retreat. After peace was proclaimed, they told him that they never wished to kill him, but wanted to rob him of his gun and watch, and carry off a negro woman of his, to raise corn for them.

But these were the early settlers, who conciliated the Indians. Those who followed, were less careful in the observance of the Golden Rule. Not understanding, nor caring to understand, that the Indian's nature is a gentle one, and best wielded by kind treatment, unintentional, and too often purposed, offence was given. The French, who were contending with the English for the possession of the Ohio Valley, fanned their discontent into open rupture. They saw, with jealousy, houses and white faces where, before, were favorite hunting-grounds. The well-known coverts supplying the certain game, were levelled to the plough. They saw themselves every day poorer, and the means of subsistence more difficult to obtain, while their white neighbors increased their own stores of corn and cattle to abundance. With this perverted state of feeling, it was easy to magnify cold manner into fancied slight, and a deserved rebuff into aggravated insult.

The settlements were sparsely scattered through the Kittatinny country. At first, the danger did not appear serious, and the people remained on their farms, though with some misgivings of entire safety. Soon abductions became frequent, and, occasionally a murder was committed, and houses and grain-stacks fired. Yet these were regarded rather as tokens of personal malice than national hostility, and, as such, insufficient cause for war.

About the year 1753, the French had succeeded in instilling in the minds of the various tribes, a hatred which nothing but blood would satisfy. The amicable feeling toward the English, that for more than thirty years had pervaded them, was now totally gone. They were laying waste portions of Virginia; and the frontier of Cumberland County[1] offered the next nearest field. Consternation was depicted on every face. Those who had been treated by the aborigines with frankness, and who expected to unmolestedly pursue their peaceful avocations, saw the uselessness of further risk. Friends and foes shared alike the savage vindictiveness.

[1] In 1750 Lancaster County was divided, and the new part took the name of Cumberland, which latter was the sixth in order of erection. Franklin County was the thirteenth in order, and was established in 1784, out of the southwestern part of Cumberland.

Colonel Washington marched with troops across the mountains against the advancing allied French and Indians, but was compelled to capitulate to superior force at Fort Necessity on the 3d July, 1754. Affairs in the valley were thrown into deplorable confusion; and petitions for relief were sent to the Provincial government.

"To the Honourable James Hamilton, Esq., Lieutenant-Governour and Commander-in-Chief of the Province of Pennsylvania and Counties of New Castle, Kent, and Sussex on Delaware.

"The address of the subscribers, Inhabitants of the County of Cumberland, humbly sheweth:

"That we are now in the most imminent danger by a powerful army of cruel, merciless, and inhuman enemies, by whom our lives, liberties, and estates, and all that tends to promote our welfare, are in the utmost danger of dreadful destruction, and this lamentable truth is most evident from the late defeat of the Virginia forces; and now, as we are under your Honour's protection, we would beg your immediate notice—we living upon the frontiers of the Province, and our enemies so close upon us—nothing doubting but that these considerations will affect your Honour, and, as you have our welfare at heart, that you defer nothing that may tend to hasten our relief," &c.[1]

Signed by BENJAMIN CHAMBERS, *and seventy-four others.*

"CUMBERLAND, July 15, 1754."

[1] Col. Rec., vol. vi. p. 130.

Throughout the year, massacres were frequent. Many farms were deserted outright. The people collected in numbers for greater safety, and tended their fields, while others watched, guns in hand, to give the alarm on the approach of danger.

Meanwhile, they were sustained in the hour of peril by the hope that the forces then being conducted to repel the enemy would be successful. The prayers of the distressed inhabitants were daily offered in their behalf. Their property, their sustenance, and their lives, depended on the fate of the expedition.

They were doomed to bitter disappointment. The news of Braddock's defeat, on the 9th July, 1755, travelled with the usual celerity of evil tidings. This overwhelming disaster completed the dismay that before had been partial only. The settlements which were causing the fertile valleys reaching toward the Ohio to smile with luxuriant crops, and the sturdy forest to bend to the blows of the civilizing axe, were abandoned in utter despair. The Indians of the further slope of the Alleghanies, ever ready for outrage, and instigated, and even led by the French, who, in the first flush of victory, miscalculated their ultimate strength, spared neither the lives nor the substance of the hated English. The people fled with what effects they could carry, to the safety afforded at Shippensburg and Carlisle. At the former town, a fort was in process of completion. Such was the urgency to put it in a defensible condition that the ring of hammers, and the labors of the men, intruded on the sacredness of the Sabbath. The town was crowded with refugees. So fierce was this war that in 1763, eight years later, there were in Shippensburg, nearly fourteen hundred of these wretched, houseless creatures occupying cellars, sheds, barns, and other outhouses; for the dwellings proper were filled to overflowing.

Another petition went from Cumberland County; and letters were written, showing the unprotected state of the frontier:—

"To the Honourable Robert Hunter Morris, Esq., Governor and Commander-in-Chief in and over the Province of Pennsylvania.

"The Humble Petition of A Number of the Inhabitants of Cumberland County, Heartily joined as a Company, Under the Care and Command of Joseph Armstrong, Esq'r, Sheweth:

"That Your Petitioners are at present in a most Dangerous Situation, as we live upon the frontier, Exposed to the Inhuman Cruelty of Barbarous Savages, and Nothing to Impede them or Defend us but the Sovereign Benignity of Almighty God, for we are in a Defenceless Condition having neither Arms nor Amunition, and in this Lamentable Case, Our Only Door of Hope (Next to the Divine Goodness) is in Your Honour's Compassion, and the more for that you have given the Utmost assurance to us of Your Care of this Province, and, in Particular, by the Late Provisions made for our Brethren in Potter's Township, who are in Equal Jeopardy with us.

"May it therefore Pleas Your Honour to Consider Our Case, and grant us Some relief, by Ordering to us such A number of Guns and Quantity of Amunition, and Upon

Such terms as Your Honour shall appoint, and Your Petitioners, as in Duty bound, shall Ever Pray.[1]

"AUGUST 7, 1755."

"FALLING SPRING, SABBATH MORNING, Nov. 2, 1755.

"To the inhabitants of the lower part of the County of Cumberland—

"GENTLEMEN: If you intend to go to the assistance of your neighbors, you need wait no longer for the certainty of the news. The Great Cove[2] is destroyed. James Campbell left his company last night, and went to the fort at Mr. Steel's meeting-house,[3] and there saw some of the inhabitants of the Great Cove, who gave this account; that as they came over the Hill, they saw their houses in flames. The messenger says that there are but one hundred, and that they are divided into two parts, the one part to go against the Cove, and the other against the Conolloways; and there are two French among them. They are Delawares and Shawnese. The part that came against the Cove are under the command of Shingas, the Delaware king. The people

[1] Pa. Archives, vol. ii. p. 385.

[2] The Great and Little Coves are valleys inclosed by mountain-spurs in the western part of Cumberland, (now Franklin) County. The first is about twenty-five, the latter about seventeen, miles from Chambersburg.

[3] One of the first forts in the Conococheague settlement was built in 1755. This stood south of Fort Loudoun about five miles, and east of Mercersburg three miles, where was situated the Presbyterian White Church. It was called "Mr. Steel's Meeting-House" for the pastor who took charge in 1754. The church, surrounded by a rude, but strong, stockade, thus became a bulwark for material, as well as spiritual, defence.

of the Cove that came off saw several men lying dead; they heard the murder shout, and the firing of guns, and saw the Indians going into their houses before they left sight of the Cove. I have sent express to Marsh Creek at the same time I send this, so I expect there will be a good company there this day; and, as there are but one hundred of the enemy, I think it is in our power, if God permit, to put them to flight if you turn out well from your parts. I understand that the West settlement is designed to go if they can get any assistance to repel them. All in haste from

Your humble servant,
BENJAMIN CHAMBERS."

Extract of a letter from Col. Jno. Armstrong to Governor Morris:—

CARLISLE, November 2, 1755.

"The two Delawares who brought the hatchet further said; That about twenty-one days ago a large number of Indians, and about one hundred French, supposed to make about fifteen hundred men, set out from Fort Du Quesne in order to destroy as many of the inhabitants eastward of the Alleghany hills as they could, and that eight days before the main body left the fort, scouting parties were sent out before them. * * * * We should be prepared to receive them every hour, for that they were certainly nigh us.

"At four o'clock this afternoon, by express from Conococheague, we are informed that yesterday about 100 Indians were seen in the Great Cove, among whom was

Shingas, the Delaware king; that immediately after the discovery, as many as had notice fled, and, looking back from an high hill, they beheld their houses on fire, heard several guns fired, and the last shrieks of their dying neighbors. * * * * Mr. Hamilton was here, with sixty men from York County, when the express came, and is to march early to-morrow to the upper part of the county. We have sent out expresses everywhere, and intend to collect the forces of this lower part, expecting the enemy every moment at Shearman's Valley, if not nearer hand. I'm of opinion that no other means than a chain of block-houses along or near the south side of the Kittatinny mountains, from the Susquehanna to the Temporary Line, can secure the lives and properties even of the old inhabitants of this county; the new settlements being all fled except Shearman's Valley, whom (if God do not preserve) we fear will suffer very soon.

I am your Honor's

disconsolate, humble servant,

JOHN ARMSTRONG."[1]

Early in 1756, "A plan for the defence of Cumberland County" was adopted, as suggested by Col. John Armstrong in his letter just quoted. Governor Morris wrote to Col. Washington:—

"FEB. 2, 1756.

"SIR: I am favored with yours of the 1st (?) instant, which I did not receive till my return on Wednesday last

[1] Pa. Archives, vol. ii. p. 452.

from the frontiers, where I have been employed for a month past in forming a line of forts and block-houses from Delaware, along the Kittatinny hills, as far as the new road that leads to the Alleghany hills, and which I am in hopes ten days will complete. On the west of Susquehanna, I have placed one at the Sugar Cabins upon the new road, which I have named Fort Lyttleton,[1] another at Aughwick, called Fort Shirley,[2] a third upon the Juniata, where the Kishequokilis[3] falls into it, called Fort Granville, and a fourth between that and the Susquehanna, called Pomfret Castle.[4] In these, I have placed garrisons of seventy-five men each, with orders to range the woods each way from their respective forts, to give notice of the approach of any enemy, and to use their utmost endeavors to intercept and destroy any parties of French and Indians they may discover."

These forts were productive of good, but were limited in their range of benefit, and left many places at the mercy of the foe. In various parts of the valley, private forts were

[1] The location of Fort Lyttleton is sixteen miles from Loudoun, or about thirty miles in a western direction from Chambersburg.

[2] Fort Shirley was at the present site of the town of Shirleysburg.

[3] "Gischochgokwalis—the snakes have all got into their dens. From the words *gischi*, already; *achgook*, snakes; *walicu*, in dens."—*Heckewelder.*

[4] Pomfret Castle was on the river *Matchitongo*, about twelve miles from the Susquehanna.

For these forts, see Gov. Morris's letters, Pa. Arch., vol. ii., pp. 556, 564, &c.

built and resorted to by those who could not reach the provincial posts. The Great and Little Coves, and the Conolloways to the west of Falling Spring, were reduced to ashes; and the inhabitants, leaving fifty prisoners in the hands of the savages, fled, some to York County, and others to Maryland. The country, for thirty miles, was laid waste; cattle were killed or driven off, and the corn rotted on the ground, for no one was left to gather it.

The petition from Falling Spring was unanswered. The same piteous appeal went up from all parts of the border. Money was difficult to raise by taxing a people struggling for precarious existence; and the government was therefore unable to comply with the urgent demands on its impoverished treasury. It could only recommend refuge in its few posts, or abandonment of the country.

Mr. Chambers was remotely situated, and beyond the immediate protection of any fort. The danger became daily more imminent. His mills, his farm, and the improvements of his neighbors, were of too much value, and had been obtained at too great a cost of labor and backwoods' privation, to leave to the despoilers.

He saw the madness of further dependence on a helpless government. The time had come for decisive resistance or ignominious flight. But one course presented itself to his entire commendation. His enterprise and industry had originated the settlement, and placed him pecuniarily at its head; and he proved himself equal to the emergency, by resolving to remain and defend it.

He built a large stone house, two stories in height, and roofed it with lead, to prevent its being fired by arrows carrying combustible matter. The walls were of great thickness, and proof against the blows of the ponderous log battering-ram. The windows were narrow, and arranged to serve as loop-holes for musketry. One corner of the fort projected over the brook to provide an unfailing supply of water in the event of a long siege—and a broad and deep moat surrounding, fed by the Falling Spring, gave increased immunity. He then inclosed this and the mills with a high stockade of upright, wooden puncheons, firmly imbedded in the ground, which formed of itself a wall of more than ordinary protection. Then, with two cannons of four pound calibre, and small arms, for offensive operations, he deemed himself quite secure. The reverberation of the report of these cannon through the lonely hills, struck terror in the hearts of the unsuccessful scalp-loving assailants of this stronghold, and the exaggerated stories of their extraordinary power, soon taught them to make no further attempts.

The vicinity of the fort, however, was closely beset; for the timorous excursions of those who had sought shelter within its hospitable walls, to the adjacent fields, would often result in a loss of the number by the fatal tomahawk, or by being carried away prisoners, subjected to all the horrors of barbarian warfare.

The alarm became general. In York County, much

nearer the Delaware river than the Conococheague part of Cumberland County, the people were ill at ease, as the following paper, read in Colonial Council, August 28, 1756, will show :—

To Governor Morris—

"The Petition of the Inhabitants of the Town and County of York, most humbly sheweth :—

"That your Petitioners are sensible that your Honour has left no measures (in your power) untried, for the protection of our lives and liberties from the outrages of a barbarous and savage enemy.

"That your petitioners hoped their sufferings were at an end when a chain of forts were erected along the frontier for their defence.

"That, notwithstanding this, skirmishes are made, murders and captivities daily committed upon the poor remaining inhabitants, who hold their possessions in the most eminent danger, in hopes of seeing more happy days.

"That all our prospects of safety and protection are now vanished, by finding one of our best forts upon the frontier burnt and destroyed, and the men who bravely defended it, carried into barbarous captivity, (and the rest of the forts liable to the same fate, which may unhappily be the case before this can reach your Honour's hands.)

"That, as the County of Cumberland is mostly evacuated, and part of this become the frontier, the enemy may easily enter and take possession of provisions sufficient to supply many thousand men, and be thereby enabled to carry their hostilities even to the metropolis. * * *

"Your petitioners therefore most humbly pray that * * your Honour will recommend our complicated distresses to the Right Honourable the Earl of Loudoun, who, upon knowing our truly deplorable condition, may be graciously pleased to take some measures to ease our calamities; perhaps to command the recruits now raised in the province, for the Royal American regiment to be forthwith sent to our relief, whilst the provincials now in pay, may go against the enemy to avenge our bleeding cause."

The Rev. John Steel, captain of a company in the pay of the province, stationed twelve miles from Falling Spring, writes, Sept. 6, 1756, to the governor, of the most miserable condition of the upper part of Cumberland County. A letter from Shippensburg, of the same month, sets forth the grievances of that town, and offers to finish a fort if allowed arms and ammunition to defend it. Official statements of that time, also represent that where, a year before, were three thousand men fit to bear arms, now, exclusive of the colonial forces, not one hundred remained.

It seems that these private forts were considered unsafe, and of no importance, by the authorities. This may have been owing to the capture and destruction of several of them, with the inmates. One provincial fort (Granville) was also overpowered.

Commissary James Young, on a tour of duty some months after the establishment of Chambers' fort, drew conclusions in reference to its strength that facts did not seem to warrant.

In a letter to Gov. Denny, he says—

"HARRIS' FERRY, Oct. 17th, 1756.

* * In our journey to Fort Littleton, we stopped at Mr. Chambers' mill, ten miles beyond Shippensburg, towards McDowell's,[1] where he has a good private fort, and on an exceeding good situation, to be made very defenceable, but what I think of great consequence to the Government is, that in said fort are two four-pound cannon mounted, and nobody but a few country people to defend it. If the enemy should take that fort, they would naturally bring those cannon to bear against Shippensburg and Carlisle. I therefore would presume to recommend it to your Honour, either to have the cannon taken from thence, or a proper garrison stationed there."[2]

The Governor being either unable or indisposed to station troops there, Mr. Chambers was applied to by the commanding officer of the department, for the delivery of the guns.

Receiving no protection, and relying on himself for success, he had encountered the multifarious dangers incident to his settlement; and when his prudence suggested, and his private funds paid for, the means of defence which the government failed to supply, official interference was not

[1] This was a private fort, erected early in 1756, and before the erection of Fort Loudoun. Being near the passes through the western mountains, it was sometimes occupied by companies of rangers and other provincial forces. It was about two miles south of Loudoun, and where the village of Bridgeport is now situated.

[2] Pa. Archives, vol. iii. p. 12.

only ill-timed, but an impugnment of his bravery and strength. The ire of the independent spirits of Conococheague was aroused at this proposal to strip them of their sole reliance while staying in possession of their homes; and they united in sustaining Mr. Chambers in his determination to resist the attempt to deprive him of them. He indignantly refused to obey an order so uncalled for, so insulting, and replied, that if he was able to build a fort and to arm it, he well knew how to defend it, and that, by superior force alone should the cannon be removed.

He was reported to the Governor. A true statement of the case could hardly have been made. If otherwise, personal enmity must have entered the matter. Mr. Chambers was one of the commissioners to locate the county-seat of Cumberland. Carlisle, Shippensburg, and a place ten miles from Falling Spring, were looked at, and the former was chosen. This made him obnoxious to those who did not succeed, for he was strenuous in favor of Carlisle; and it is possible that the governor's mind was biassed by partial representations of those opposed to Chambers.

Col. John Armstrong, in a letter to Gov. Denny, of the date of November 30, 1756, says—

"I have written to Mr. Chambers, concerning the guns at his Fort, according to order, but he thinks, by going to Philadelphia, he may prevail with y^r^ Hon^r^ to let them stay where they are, and is to set out for that purpose in a few days."[1]

[1] Pa. Archives, vol. iii. p. 77.

Be the cause what it may, the offence was too flagrant an act of insubordination to pass unnoticed; and, despite the propriety of retaining the guns, the Governor proceeded to administer a lesson of obedience in the following summons :—

Pennsylvania, *ss.*

The Honourable William Denny, Esquire, Lieutenant Governor & Commander in Chief of the Province of Pennsylvania and Counties of Newcastle, Kent and Sussex on Delaware. To the Sheriff of Cumberland County Greeting. Whereas it having been represented to me that two Great Guns or Cannon were in the Custody and Possession of a Certain Benjamin Chambers at his Dwelling House on the Western Frontier of this Province in the said County of Cumberland, Where they did lie exposed to his Majesty's Enemies who by taking Possession of them might thereby be the better enabled to annoy and Distress his said Majesty's Subjects in this Province, and to lay Siege to and reduce his Majesty's Forts. Therein moved by my Duty to my Sovereign, and a regard & concern for the safety of the People of this Province under my Command, care and Protection. I issued my Order in writing bearing date on or about the fourth day of February last past, directed to Lieutenant Colonel John Armstrong, thereby Commanding him to cause the said two Cannon to be removed from the dwelling House of the said Benjamin Chambers to Shippensburg or some other Fort under his Command as a place of safety, where they might be secure from falling into the hands of the Enemy. And Whereas it has been proved to my satisfaction that the said John Armstrong did send a party of his Majesty's Forces under the Command of Thomas Smallman, to remove the said Cannon accordingly, and that the said Benjamin Chambers with an intent to disturb the King's peace himself did assemble with divers other Persons unknown armed with Swords, Guns, and other Warlike weapons, and Riotously, Traitorously and Seditiously without any Lawful authority did oppose the March of the said Thomas Smallman and the other Forces under his Command, would not suffer them to execute my said order, and did not only refuse to deliver up the said Cannon, but did threaten to kill the said Thomas or any of the said Forces who should offer to take Possession of the said Cannon, and I have reason to believe that the said Benjamin Chambers is disaffected to his Majesty and his Government. You are therefore hereby strictly charged and commanded to take the Body of the said Benjamin Chambers, and bring him under a strong Guard before me the said William Denny, Esquire, at the City of Philadelphia, to answer the Premises and be dealt with according to Law, and all Officers Civil and Military, and others his Majesty's Subjects in this Province are hereby ordered and charged to be aiding and assisting to you therein. Hereof fail not, as you will answer the Contrary at your Peril, and for your so doing this Shall be your Warrant, Given under my Hand and Seal at Arms at Philadelphia the fifth day of April, & Thirtieth Year of his Majesty's Reign.

WILLIAM DENNY."[1]

[1] Pa. Archives, vol. iii. p. 105.

Col. Armstrong was deputed to convey the order into effect. He found the settlers still firm in the resolve to keep the guns. Irritated at seeing his authority disregarded, and his force inadequate to the seizure of them, he wrote as follows:—

"CARLISLE, 30th June, 1757.

* * I'm sorry Mr. Allen should be so uneasy on the score of a person so troublesome and so perverse as Chambers is known to be; the recognizance was not taken for his appearance before any person but the governor, who issued the writ; it's thought, Chambers now designs a law-suit, and he has said the action will be brought against me, where I think it cannot lie.

If it is found, that he designs trouble (as he has the brass and malice of the Devil) I think the Governor should write to Col. Stanwix; in the mean time, I will open the matter to the colonel, who may think it necessary to seize the guns himself. I am conscious he was, on that occasion, treated not only with justice, but also with lenity. * *

* * The old magistrates had no other reason for resigning than lest they should be left out; though some of them I have lately heard say, it was owing to the Governor's treatment of Ben. Chambers in regard of his guns; but this is finesse."[1] * * * *

How the dispute ended is not known; but the best refutation of Commissary Young's fears, and evidence of the completeness of the defensive plans are, that Mr. Cham-

[1] Pa. Archives, vol. iii. p. 192.

bers remained in his fort during the eight years' war that depopulated the country around. That the "two Great Guns" were not removed, is apparent from the circumstance of one of them being used at Chambersburg seventy-three years after it had assisted in repelling the foes of England, in the celebration of the anniversary of Independence Day.

THE OLD CHURCHYARD.

In 1764, the town of Chambersburg was regularly surveyed. At one end of it, lay secluded a romantic prominence of a few acres in extent. This was conveyed, in 1768, through deed of gift, by Benjamin Chambers and wife, to the religious society "then and thereafter adhering to the Westminster profession of faith, and the mode of government therein contained," for the purposes of a house of worship, session and school-houses, and cemetery. The congregation of Falling Spring was organized in 1738, and incorporated by act of Assembly, in 1787.

A hundred feet or more from the road that skirts the front of this ground, on the summit of the gradual rise, a small log church was built.

"Here were they gathered every good Lord's day,
From town, from hamlet, and from country wide,
In pleasant groups, but meek and staid alway,
They showed not often levity nor pride.
* * * * * *
Blest sight it was to mark that Godly flock,
At intermission, grouped throughout this wood.
Each log, each bench, each family upping-block,
Some granddame held amidst her gathered brood.
Here cakes were shared, and fruit, and counsel good;
Devoutly spoken, 'twas of crops and rain;
Hard by the church the broad-brimmed elders stood,
While o'er that slope did flow a constant train
Of bevies, springward bound, or coming back again."

When the audience was beyond the capacity of the church, service was held, in pleasant weather, at the mill, in which, and in the cool shade of the surrounding trees, benches were ranged. In 1767, to accommodate the increased number of hearers, it was replaced by a large, single-storied house, framed by joining three lengths of logs end to end, and was of considerable width. This stood until 1803, when the present substantial stone edifice was erected.[1]

[1] It is surprising to note the want, in those days, of the commonest articles of utility. An extract from the minutes of this congregation will give a curious and interesting illustration.

"2ND MEETING, WEDNESDAY, 8th of February, 1786.

"Mr. Martin proposed to make a book for the Purpose of opening a New account with the Subscribers in the Congregation upon which it was ordered that Mr. James Moor Purchase three quires of Paper of John Colhoon and deliver the same to Mr. Martin for this Purpose and Pay the same out of Monies of the Congregation now remaining in his Possession.

"Mr. Edward Crawford is appointed to purchase three quires of Paper and to make the same into a Book and transcribe the act of Incorporation into the beginning of the same to be delivered to the Secretary at our next meeting for the use of the Trustees.

"3RD MEETING, MARCH 21st, 1786.

"The Trustees met according to their adjournment. Present the Rev. James Lang, Col. Benjamin Chambers, James Moor, Matthew Wilson, Patrick Varin and Josiah Crawford. Began with Prayer.

"Mr. James Moor found on application to John Colhoon for Paper to make the Book as directed at our last meeting, that there was none that would suit. So the Book is not yet provided. Mr. Moor is ordered to provide the Paper for this Purpose as soon as possible.

"Mr. Edward Crawford Junr. not being present, there is no account

From the rear of the church, the ground falls rapidly to a grass-grown ravine, once the bed of the brook, but diverted long ago into its present course by a beaver-dam. Across this, an embankment has been made for convenient transit to the main portion of the cemetery, which is broad and level, and terminates abruptly in a low bluff, thickly set with bushes. By its base the dark-brown waters of the Conococheague flow gently in ripple and mirroring sheet, and under which, in the alternating disclosure and obscurity of the drifting clouds, can be seen ridges of rich deposite and gray sand at the bottom. Huge slaty masses shelve from the opposite shore far into the stream; and against them the white-crested waves exhaust their puny strength in rapid succession, and in well-defined line of evanescing bubbles and yeasty foam float slowly out of view.

The plateau is studded with clumps of mournful cedars, whose sombre green hue and prim outline are thrown into agreeable contrast by the bright walnut-leaves in the sere and yellow of annual mutation, and more delicate and fringe-like in juxtaposition with the gnarled arms and early frost-tinted foliage of the spreading oak. Out over the creek the eye ranges on multiplied hill and woody

whether he hath fulfilled his appointment respecting the Book for the use of the Board."

Not long after this, Dr. Colhoon started at Chambersburg the first paper mill in the valley, if not in the western country. From this point, paper was supplied as late as 1817 by means of pack horses, and then by wagons, to Pittsburg and adjacent districts. An early issue of a Pittsburg journal contains an apology for its delay because the paper from Chambersburg had not arrived in its usual time.

dale until they confusedly blend in the distant Kittatinny Mountain.

In other directions, the density of the immediate forest precludes the noise and sight of busy outer cares, and impresses the wanderer within its limits with the gloom of desolation. It is a spot where the world, so lately radiant with the hopes and fears and sweet experiences that animate us to continued exertion, relapses into the merest dream of reality—where the futility of earthly aspirations, compared with the glowing prize of immortality, overwhelms and saddens; and retrospective musings, admit no consolatory anticipations for the future.

Appropriately situated in the depths of this solitude, in a low stone inclosure, whose antiquated architecture bespeaks the work of a past generation, is the gathering-place in death of the Chambers family. There rests a pioneer of 1730; by his side lie two of his sons—a brave colonel and a gallant captain of the Revolution; near them now, as in life, a true Christian wife and mother, and others, whom but to name invoke our tearful homage; while, close by, a plain white shaft, spotless and of recent erection, marks the entombment of the crushed hopes and the heart-wrung solicitude that were centered in an only son.

Through the dreary black winter night the old trees creak and bend to the furious blast in such strange notes, that we seem almost to hear again the wild pibroch wail that in direful days of yore collected the Scottish clans to battle undismayed for the right. At other times, the balmy autumnal evening breeze sighs through the rustling leaves a requiem gushing full of melody and soothing sweetness, until we feel that though alone in the abode of the dead, we can again commune with those we most loved. Amid the swaying of the pensile boughs of this sacred wood we silently ponder over the cold marble that tells in few brief lines the beginning and the ending of some of those who toiled and wearied not in the good fight of faith and liberty in the Cumberland valley—who for opinion's sake risked their lives and their fortunes for a home of free thought in this distant land of promise.

It is not difficult to imagine the emotions with which the provident giver of this holy ground foresaw the common benefit of his appropriation, nor fail to appreciate the gentle pathos of the sentiment that exacted in return the yearly presentation in the month of June of a single rose. This affecting and beautiful ceremony, it need hardly be added, was piously observed for a long period.

Of this Falling Spring congregation, Benjamin Chambers was an active and an humble member, for he lived in the fear and the love of the Redeemer. His death, in 1788, was calm and joyous; and in the cemetery he so tenderly regarded, sleep the remains of the first white settler of that vicinity.

THE REVOLUTION.

Patriotism was ever a leading trait among the people of the Kittatinny Valley. As borderers, and as provincial troops throughout the old French war and the subsequent harassing Indian war, and as independent maintainers of their isolated positions, they were conspicuous in bearing the severest portion of the defence of the frontier.

It is a prevalent idea, and much dwelt upon, that those who pronounced for liberty in 1775 were its authors. This perhaps is right; yet they but gave expression to the awakened instincts of an intelligent people. It is urged, and with much plausibility, that no evidence exists of such previously-entertained aims. Were this even so, it would prove but little; for no one then cared to rashly incur the penalties of treason by publishing his opposition to the supreme government.

That this dream of independence floated through the popular mind long ere its national existence is clearly apparent. Prior to the Revolution are to be found allusions—in the English interest, and, of course, adverse to the feasibility of independence—showing that the idea at least was cherished. This was the legitimate result of living at great distance from a chief government, which the colonists knew only as the source of capricious and exacting officials, by whom the best energies of a country capable of self-maintenance, and withal increasing in vigor, were taxed without receiving the benefit therefrom.

Conclusive on this head is the negative evidence, in 1755, of Lewis Evans, of Philadelphia (and his is probably the first record of alarming dissatisfaction):—"It would be the height of madness for them to propose an Independency."[1] Twenty brief years saw the culmination of that madness, and but little imagination is requisite to fancy the turbulent Pennsylvanians chafing the estimable geographer into his emphatic argument. Not less so is James Maury, who wrote in 1756: "We have been informed that such accounts of our temper and disposition in this colony (Virginia) have been transmitted to England by a certain person that the Ministry suppose we want nothing but ability and opportunity to attempt shaking off allegiance."[2]

Thus it is manifest that the sentiment of liberty was not sprung as a sudden or individual creation on the public gaze. It was latent and deep-seated, and had vigorous root in the affections of the people. More quick to move than those who become the exponents of the popular will, the people are always in advance. It is only when the masses are ripe for action that the feeling finds vent in the prominent few. Without this solid basis, attempt at leadership becomes mere personal advancement, and the hero or patriot degenerates to the paltry factionist or traitor.

[1] Analysis of a general map of the Colonies, p. 32.

[2] Memoirs of a Huguenot Family, p. 405.

Had not the simultaneous passage of resolutions throughout the colonies been concerted, and, in fact proposed, by the Committees of Correspondence, it is not too much to believe that the hereditary sense of right, which had so long animated this people, and which was kept in abeyance by the wisdom that saw defeat in premature action, signal success in unity, would have led to the immediate defiant avowal of independence.[1]

[1] The subjoined resolutions are similar to those of various meetings held through the colonies; and, as designed by the Committees of Correspondence, they emboldened the congress that met in Philadelphia the September following to adopt the decisive measures put forth by them.

"At a respectable meeting of the freeholders and freemen from several townships of the Cumberland County in the province of Pennsylvania, held at Carlisle in the said county, on Tuesday the 12th day of July, 1774; John Montgomery, Esq., in the chair.

1. Resolved, That the late act of the parliament of Great Britain, by which the port of Boston is shut up, is oppressive to that town, and subversive of the rights and liberties of the Colony of Massachusetts Bay; that the principle upon which that act is founded is not more subversive of the rights and liberties of that colony than it is of all other British colonies in North America; and, therefore, the inhabitants of Boston are suffering in the common cause of all these colonies.

2. That every vigorous and prudent measure ought speedily and unanimously to be adopted by these colonies for obtaining redress of the grievances under which the inhabitants of Boston are now laboring; and security from grievance of the same or of a still more severe nature, under which they and the other inhabitants of the colonies may, by a further operation of the same principle, hereafter labor.

3. That a Congress of Deputies from all the colonies will be one proper method for obtaining these purposes.

4. That the same purposes will, in the opinion of this meeting, be promoted by an agreement of all the colonies not to import any mer-

Pennsylvania was a fitting school for the coming glorious struggle. Side by side, for a series of years against the common enemy, the comparative merits of English and American arms were tested; but not until the bitter lesson on the fatal field of Monongahela was the invidious distinction broadly and irremediably drawn. In this long-continued border warfare, irregular and peculiar by reason of the habits and character of the aborigines, and perfected by arduous experience, was acquired a degree of

chandize from nor export any merchandize to Great Britain, Ireland, or the British West Indies, nor to use any such merchandize so imported, nor tea imported from any place whatever till these purposes shall be obtained; but that the inhabitants of this county will join any restriction of that agreement which the General Congress may think it necessary for the colonies to confine themselves to.

5. That the inhabitants of this county will contribute to the relief of their suffering brethren in Boston at any time when they shall receive intimation that such relief will be most seasonable.

6. That a committee be immediately appointed for this county, to correspond with the committee of this province, or of the other provinces, upon the great objects of the public attention; and to co-operate in every measure conducing to the general welfare of British America.

7. That the committee consist of the following persons, viz: James Wilson, John Armstrong, John Montgomery, William Irvine, Robert Callender, William Thompson, John Colhoon, Jonathan Hoge, Robert Magaw, Ephraim Blane, John Allison, John Harris, and Robert Miller, or any five of them.

8. That James Wilson, Robert Magaw, and William Irvine be the Deputies appointed to meet the Deputies from other counties of this province at Philadelphia, on Friday next, in order to concert measures preparatory to the General Congress."* JOHN MONTGOMERY, *Chairman.*

---

* Rupp, p. 403, *et seq.*

native self-reliance which soon taught the Americans the superiority of their tactics over those of the most approved European generalship, and at the same time showed them what to expect in the event of separation.

At the commencement of the Revolution, Mr. Chambers was unfit, by infirmity of years, for the fatigues and exposure of a campaign so distant as the heights of Boston. But the spirit which in his progenitors resisted with zealous bravery, arbitrary power in Ireland and Scotland had, by the process of transplanting to the savage wilds of America, lost none of its devotion to just principles of government.

On the receipt of the news of the battle of Lexington, commendatory meetings were held, and the people banded together in opposition to unmerited aggression.[1]

[1] A gentleman writing from Carlisle, May 6, 1775, says—

"Yesterday the County Committee met from nineteen townships on the short notice they had. About three thousand men have already associated. The arms returned amount to about fifteen hundred. The committee have voted five hundred effective men, besides commissioned officers, to be immediately drafted, taken into pay, armed and disciplined, to march on the first emergency; to be paid and supported as long as necessary by a tax on all estates, real and personal, in the county; the returns to be taken by the township committees; and the tax laid by the commissioners and assessors; the pay of the officers and men as usual in times past.

"This morning we met again at eight o'clock; among other subjects

Mr. Chambers' eldest son, James, was an ardent supporter of the rebel cause. In June, 1775, he marched as captain of a company of infantry, accompanied by his brothers, William and Benjamin, as cadets, to the siege of Boston.[1]

The ensuing extracts from James Chambers' private correspondence (mostly to his wife) present stirring pictures of some of the important events of the period to which they relate. They will be welcomed by the patriot reader to the reminiscences of the Revolution, and by the

of inquiry this day, the mode of drafting, or taking into pay, arming and victualling immediately the men, and the choice of field and other officers, will, among other matters, be the subject of deliberation. The strength or spirit of this county perhaps may appear small if judged by the number of men proposed; but when it is considered that we are ready to raise fifteen hundred or two thousand, should we have support from the Province, and that independent, and in uncertain expectation of support, we have voluntarily drawn upon this county a debt of about £27,000 per annum, I hope we shall not appear contemptible. We make great improvements in military discipline. It is yet uncertain who may go."—*Am. Archives*, ii. 516.

[1] William and Benjamin Chambers were respectively twenty-two and twenty years of age at this time. They were advanced to the rank of captain soon after they joined the army. They were at the battles of Long Island, Brandywine, and Germantown, and encountered the severities of the campaign of 1776 and 1777 in the Jerseys. They, however, returned home before the close of the war to the attention of their aged parents and their property, which latter had suffered greatly from neglect. Notwithstanding their compulsory absence from the battle-fields of the nation, they frequently assisted in the pursuit of Indians, whose incursions on the settlements of Bedford and Huntingdon Counties created much alarm.

posterity of the participators in the momentous struggle, as most worthy of respectful registry:—

"CAMBRIDGE, AUGUST 13, 1775.

"MY DEAR KITTY: We arrived in camp on the 7th ult., about 12 o'clock. We were not here above an hour until we went to view the lines where the English camp is all in plain sight. We crossed the lines, and went beyond the outposts to a small hill, within musket-shot of a man-of-war and a floating battery, and not further from the works at the foot of Bunker Hill, where we could see them very plainly. Whilst I was standing there, some of our riflemen slipped down ——— Hill, about a gunshot to the left of us, and began firing. The Regulars returned it without hurting our men. We thought we saw one of the red coats fall. Since the riflemen came here, by the latest accounts from Boston, there have been forty-two killed, and thirty-eight prisoners taken at the Lighthouse, twelve of the latter Tories. Amongst the killed are four captains, one of them the son of a Lord, and worth £40,000 a year, whose name I cannot recollect. The riflemen go where they please, and keep the Regulars in continual hot water.

They are every day firing cannon at our people, but have not yet killed a man. We expect six wagons loaded with powder here in two or three days; and when they arrive, our twenty-four pounders will begin to play on their ships and the lines on Bunker Hill. It is difficult for our men to get within shot of them, as they have floating batteries that flank the end of Winter Hill, and men-of-war on the other side, though our boys think they killed several of them about an hour ago. I saw a small cannonading between two of the enemy's boats and one of our batteries to the north of Boston. We can see all the town distinctly from our fort on Prospect Hill, and it is a very pretty place. * * * Two deserters came to us last night."

"CAMP AT CAMBRIDGE, AUG. 29, 1775.

"MY DEAR KITTY:

* * * * * * * * *

* * "On the evening of the 26th inst., Saturday, I was ordered to draw fifty men out of each of the Cumberland companies, and be ready to march at sunset. Accordingly I did so, and marched without beat of drum to Prospect Hill, and thence proceeded with the riflemen stationed there—in all about four hundred;—to Ploughed Hill and then down the hill within three or four hundred yards of the enemy's strongest works, to cover a party of about two thousand musketmen, who were at the same time to entrench on Ploughed Hill.

They labored very hard all night, and at daybreak had the redoubt nearly completed. When the English discovered our defences so near, they began a heavy cannonading which continued all day. They killed with their cannon balls one adjutant and one soldier, and wounded three others with musket balls. These were close to the floating batteries and their field works. Mr. William Simpson of Paxton, a volunteer, was struck by a shot and his foot carried away.

On Monday we were with about fifteen thousand men on Ploughed Hill, as the enemy made every appearance of coming out to storm our works, but thought it not good for their health, and so returned to Boston. They fired several cannon from Bunker Hill, and killed one man on Ploughed Hill. This last point is about six hundred yards from Bunker's, where is their strongest force. Your son Benjamin sends his love to you. He was with me in all this affair."

On March 7th, 1776, the Continental Congress promoted Captain Chambers to the lieutenant colonelcy of "Hand's Rifle Battalion in the Army at Cambridge." He was soon after ordered to the vicinity of New York. The following was written after the battle of Long Island. His commission of colonel of the 1st regiment of continental troops of the Pennsylvania Line is dated September 26th, 1776.

"IN CAMP AT DELAMERE'S MILLS, *three miles above King's Bridge.*

"SEPTEMBER 3, 1776.

"MY DEAR KITTY: I should have written to you sooner, but the hurry and confusion we have been in for some time past, has hindered me. I will now give you a short account of transactions in this quarter.

On the morning of the 22nd August there were nine thousand British troops on New Utrecht plains. The guard alarmed our small camp, and we assembled at the flagstaff. We marched our forces, about two hundred in number, to New Utrecht to watch the movements of the enemy. When we came on the hill, we discovered a party of them advancing toward us. We prepared to give them a warm reception, when an imprudent fellow fired, and they immediately halted and turned toward Flatbush. The main body also, moved along the great road toward the same place. We proceeded alongside of them in the edge of the woods as far as the turn of the lane, where the cherry-trees were, if you remember. We then found it impracticable for so small a force to attack them on the plain, and sent Captain Hamilton with twenty men, before them to burn all the grain; which he did very cleverly, and killed a great many cattle. It was then thought most proper to return to camp and secure our baggage, which we did, and left it in Fort Brown. Near 12 o'clock the same day we returned down the great road to Flatbush with only our small regiment, and one New England regiment sent to support us, though at a mile's distance. When in sight of Flatbush, we discovered the enemy, but not the main body; on perceiving us, they retreated down the road perhaps a mile. A party of our people commanded by Captain Miller followed them close with a design to decoy a portion of them to follow him, whilst the rest kept in the edge of the woods alongside of Captain M. But they thought better of the matter, and would not come after him though he went within two hundred yards. There they stood for a long time, and then Captain Miller turned off to us and we proceeded along their flank.

Some of our men fired upon and killed several Hessians, as we ascertained two days afterwards. Strong guards were maintained all day on the flanks of the enemy, and our regiment and the Hessian yagers kept up a severe firing, with a loss of but two wounded on our side. We laid a few Hessians low, and made them retreat out of Flatbush. Our people went into the town, and brought the goods out of the burning houses.

The enemy liked to have lost their field-pieces. Captain Steel, of your vicinity, acted bravely. We would certainly have had the cannon had it not been for some foolish person calling retreat. The main body of the foe returned to the town; and when our lads came back, they told of their exploits. This was doubted by some, which enraged our men so much that a few of them ran and brought away several Hessians on their backs. This kind of firing by our riflemen and theirs continued until ten (two?) o'clock in the morning of the 26th, when our regiment was relieved by a portion of the Flying Camp; and we started for Fort Greene to get refreshment, not having lain down the whole of this time, and almost dead with fatigue. We had just got to the fort, and I had only laid down, when the alarm guns were fired. We were compelled to turn out to the lines, and as soon as it was light saw our men and theirs engaged with field-pieces. At last, the enemy found means to surround our men there upon guard, and then a heavy firing continued for several hours. The main body that surrounded our men marched up within thirty yards of Forts Brown and Greene; but when we fired, they retreated with loss. From all I can learn, we numbered about twenty-five hundred, and the attacking party not less than twenty-five thousand, as they had been landing for days before. Our men behaved as bravely as ever men did; but it is surprising that, with the superiority of numbers, they were not cut to pieces. They behaved gallantly, and there are but five or six hundred missing.

General Lord Stirling fought like a wolf, and is taken prisoner. Colonels Miles and Atlee, Major Bird, Captain Peoples, Lieutenant Watt, and a great number of our other officers also prisoners; Colonel Piper missing. From deserters, we learn that the enemy lost Major-General Grant and two Brigadiers, and many others, and five hundred[1] killed. Our loss is chiefly in prisoners.

It was thought advisable to retreat off Long Island; and on the night of the 30th, it was done with great secrecy. Very few of the officers knew it until they were on the boats, supposing that an attack was intended. A discovery of our intention to the enemy would have been fatal to us. The Pennsylvania troops were done great honor by being chosen the *corps de reserve* to cover the retreat. The regiments of Colonels Hand,[2] Hagan, Shea, and Hazlett were detailed for that purpose. We kept up fires, with outposts stationed, until all the rest were over. We left the lines after it was fair day, and then came off.

Never was a greater feat of generalship shown than in this retreat; to bring off an army of twelve thousand men within sight of a strong enemy, possessed of as strong a

[1] 400.

[2] Chambers was lieutenant-colonel of this regiment.

fleet as ever floated on our seas, without any loss, and saving all the baggage.

General Washington saw the last over himself."

"Mount Prospect Camp, June, 1777.

* * * * * * * * *

* * This day week, we drove the enemy from Brunswick, and I was one of the first officers that entered the town. The advance party took two prisoners, one a Hessian officer. We cannonaded them smartly; and they ran, and left the works as we approached, without firing a gun, though we were within shot of small arms."

This letter, relating to the battle of Brandywine, is without date, but must have been written not long subsequent to its occurrence. Colonel Chambers' command opposed the Hessians under General Knyphausen in his strategical movement of crossing Chadd's Ford to enable Generals Howe and Cornwallis to effect a passage, with the least resistance, at the forks of the stream. In this action, the Colonel received a ball in his right side, which, though not productive of serious inconvenience at the time, by derangement of some internal function, was in later life the source of frequent and harassing illness.

"My dear—

* * * * * * * * *

* * On the morning of the 11th Sept., 1777, we were apprised that the enemy was advancing; and soon

after heard the engagement between our light troops and their advanced parties. Whilst their main design was in front to our right, the cannon ceased firing except now and then; and small detachments of our troops were constantly skirmishing with them. But in a short while, we found that they had crossed the Brandywine near the forks, and were coming in flank of our right wing. The cannonade commenced about three o'clock, but soon gave way to small arms, which continued like an incessant clap of thunder till within an hour of sunset, when our people filed off. Then the attack began with us on the left. But I must observe to you that while the right was engaged, the troops that were on the right of our brigade on the hill were drawn off * * * and left our right flank quite uncovered. The enemy kept an unremitted fire from their artillery (and ours too, played with great fury) until advancing under the thick smoke they took possession of the redoubt in front of our park.

As there were no troops to cover the artillery in the redoubt--the enemy was within thirty yards before being discovered—our men were forced to fly and to leave three pieces behind. Our brigade was drawn into line, with the park of artillery two hundred yards in the rear of the redoubt. Our park was ordered off then, and my right exposed. The enemy advanced on the hill where our park was, and came within fifty yards of the hill above me. I then ordered my men to fire. Two or three rounds made the lads clear the ground.

The General sent orders for our artillery to retreat—it was on my right—and ordered me to cover it with——

of my regiment. It was done, but to my surprise the artillerymen had run and left the howitzer behind. The two field pieces went up the road protected by about sixty of my men, who had very warm work, but brought them safe. I then ordered another party to fly to the howitzer and bring it off. Captain Buchanan, Lieutenant Stimson, and Lieutenant Douglass went immediately to the gun, and the men followed their example, and I covered them with the few I had remaining. But before this could be done, the main body of the foe came within thirty yards, and kept up the most terrible fire I suppose ever heard in America; though with very little loss on our side. I brought all the brigade artillery safely off, and I hope to see them again fired at the scoundrels. Yet we retreated to the next height in good order, in the midst of a very heavy fire of cannon and small arms. Not thirty yards distant, we formed to receive them, but they did not choose to follow.

I lost Lieutenants Halliday and Wise killed; Captain Grier was badly wounded, Captain Craig and myself slightly wounded. I have, I suppose, lost six or seven killed, and about the same number wounded. We lost several fine officers out of the brigade."

"CAMP ENGLISHTOWN, June 30th, 1778.

MY DEAR—

I have the pleasure to inform you that on the 28th ult., we gave the enemy a fine drubbing at Freehold Church,[1]

[1] This was the battle of Monmouth.

about four miles from this place. The attack commenced at eleven o'clock, and a most violent cannonade continued for nearly five hours; in which time both armies were manœuvring on the right and left. Our Division was drawn in front of our artillery in a small hollow, while the enemy's artillery was placed on an eminence in front of our brigade. Of course, we were in a right line of their fire, both parties playing their cannon over our heads, and yet only killed two of our men, and wounded four of my regiment with splinters of rails. Our army out-generalled them, and at the same time advanced some baggage across a swamp, and drove them before us. They fled in all quarters, and at sunset we had driven them near to Monmouth town. We encamped on the field that night.

They left on the ground several officers of distinction, amongst them Colonel Monckton; and yesterday we buried upwards of two hundred and fifty of the bold Britons who were to conquer the world!

I rode over the whole ground, and saw two hundred of their dead. It is surprising that we lost not more than thirty.[1] However, of this I can assure you, that for every ten of them I did not see one of ours killed. During yesterday, our fatigue parties were collecting the dead in piles, and burying them. The enemy is flying with precipitation to the Hook, and we are now on our march to Brunswick. They desert very fast, so watch for news.

J. C."

[1] The British loss was about three hundred killed in battle; the American not seventy, while both armies suffered some mortality from fatigue and the excessive heat.

Lieutenant-Colonel Harmar, Inspector of the Pennsylvania Line, wrote to President Reed, respecting the "State of the regiments comprising Major-General St. Clair's Division:"—

"CAMP, WEST POINT, October 15th, 1779.

Sir: I have the honor of transmitting your Excellency a Return of the strength of the eight regiments which at present compose the Pennsylvania Division, specifying when their times expire. The three other regiments of our Line being detached, cannot be ascertained.

As the whole army now undergoes a monthly inspection I beg leave to state to your Excellency the condition of our troops. Their clothing (which was drawn last fall at Fredericksburg) is now old and tattered. Shirts and blankets greatly wanted and scarcely a good hat in the whole division. The daily and hard fatigue at this post must consequently soon render them still worse. But notwithstanding all these inconveniences, they are well armed and cut as clean and decent an appearance as circumstances can possibly admit."[1]

By reference to the return accompanying the above report, it shows that of Chambers' regiment there were present the colonel, the lieutenant-colonel, one major, five captains, nine lieutenants, two ensigns, one surgeon, twenty-four sergeants, sixteen corporals, thirteen drums and fifes, one hundred and eighty-three privates. Total,

[1] Pa. Archives, vol. vii. p. 750.

two hundred and thirty-six. Enlisted for the war, two hundred and thirty-two; for three years, four.

Total effective force of the division, two thousand three hundred and eighty-six; non-effectives, forty-seven.

After the battle of Monmouth, Colonel Chambers was with the army at White Plains, West Point, and other parts of the country near the Hudson river. His order-books, embracing the period from July 26th, 1778, to August 5th, 1780, have lately been deposited in the library of the Society. They contain the official details of the movements of the 1st regiment and the division with which he was connected; and beyond copies of the orders relative to the attack on Bergen Point, nothing of special import to this narrative.

The following orders of General Wayne show the participation of the 1st regiment and other Pennsylvania troops in the engagement at Bergen Point, and explain Chambers' letter in reference to it.

"After Orders, New Bridge, July 21, 1780.

* * * * * * * * *

A detachment from the 1st regiment will prevent the retreat of the refugees towards Paulus Hook—whilst this is performing, the artillery will be preparing to demolish the block houses—every precaution will be used to guard against any serious consequences from up the river; and should the enemy be hardy enough to attempt the relief of this post from Fort Washington, it may add never fading laurels to troops which have always stepped the first for glory, and who have everything to expect from victory, nothing to dread from disgrace; for although it is not in their power to command success, the general is well assured they will produce a conviction to the world that they deserve it."[1]

"DIVISION ORDERS, July 23, 1780.

It is with infinite pleasure that General Wayne acknowledges to the worthy officers and soldiers under his command since the 20th inst., that he never saw more true fortitude than that exhibited on the 21st, by the troops immediately at the point of action; such was the enthusiastic bravery of all ranks of officers and men, that the 1st regiment, no longer capable of constraint, rushed with impetuosity over the abattis and up to the stockades, from which they were with difficulty withdrawn; the contagion spread to the 2d, but by the united efforts of the field and other officers of each regiment, they were at last restrained. The general fortunately would not admit of the further advance of the 10th, and the situation of General Irvine's and the other troops, prevented them from experiencing some loss of men; as the same gallant spirit pervaded the whole, they very probably would have shown the same eager desire for close action. The block house was only a

[1] Pa. Archives, vol. viii. p. 451.

secondary object, and to serve as a lure to draw the enemy across the river, and afford us an opportunity of deciding the fate of the day in the defiles through which they might pass before they could possess the strong ground. At 12 o'clock, the affairs assumed a pleasing aspect; by intelligence from Gloster that the British were embarking at Philips, and falling down the river towards Fort Lee, where the 6th and 7th regiments were posted with orders to secrete themselves, and after the enemy landed, to meet them in the gorge of the mountain, and dispute the pass with the point of the bayonet at every expense of blood, until General Irvine with the 2d, and Colonel Humpton with the 1st brigades would arrive to support them. So that there ought to be no difficulty in giving up a small object for one that was capital. Indeed, had the artillery been of sufficient calibre, the brave officers and men who conducted them would have succeeded in the reduction of the block house by a constant fire of more than one hour, within the medium distance of 60 yards, and not been under the disagreeable sensation of leaving a post unreduced behind them—this being too trifling an affair to attend to any longer, when a more ample and glorious prospect was before us; but in this we have been disappointed, as the enemy prudently chose to remain in a less hostile position than that of the Jersey shore.

The general cannot attempt to discriminate between officers, regiments or corps, who with equal opportunity would have acted with equal fortitude; and he fondly hopes that the day is not far distant when the prowess of those troops will be acknowledged by the European and American world.[1]

By order of General Wayne.
B. FISHBOURN, *Aid-de-Camp*."

"CAMP AT NEW BRIDGE, HACKENSACK, Sept. 5, 1780.

MY DEAR KITTY:

* * * * * * * * *

* * About the 20th July, General Wayne formed a design of attacking a block house built by the British on the bank of North River, on the point that runs down to Bergen, six or seven miles above that town; and had orders from the Commander in Chief to bring off the cattle. The general marched the Pennsylvania division down in the night to within a few miles of the place of action, and then in the morning ordered the 2d brigade to take post near Fort Lee, to prevent the enemy crossing from Fort Washington, and falling on the rear of the troops destined for the attack. After making the disposition necessary, my regiment was ordered to advance and commence the attack, and to cover the artillery, which was done with unparalleled bravery. Advancing to the abattis, which was within twenty yards of the house, several crept through, and there continued under an incessant fire till ordered away. They retreated with reluctance. The foe kept close under shelter, firing through loop holes. Our men and artillery kept up a galling fire on the house, but

[1] Pa. Archives, vol. viii. p. 452.

at last were obliged to fall back, as our pieces were too light to penetrate. There were twelve killed of the 1st regiment, and four of them within the abattis; in all, forty were killed, wounded and missing; three of these in Ben's platoon. You may depend your son is a good soldier. All the officers and men say he behaved exceedingly well. I had not the pleasure of seeing it, as I lay very sick at the time. Ben can tell you plenty of news about fighting.

J. C."

An act was passed by Congress to take effect January 1, 1781, reducing the Pennsylvania Line to six regiments and allowing such officers as wished it, to retire with honorable provision, exemption from various duties, &c. &c.

Colonel Chambers availed himself of this opportunity to quit the service after nearly six years' unremitting devotion to it. Colonel Brodhead of the 8th then took command of the gallant 1st regiment.

He evinced an interest in the cause before the war, as a contributor to the columns of the *Bostonian* in 1775. The annexed receipt shows that he also was a subscriber to that paper:—

"Received of James Chambers eight bushels of wheat, being his subscription to the *Bostonian*.

Jany. 7th, 1775. BENJ. CHAMBERS, JUN."

It was expected that the Colonel or his brother Benjamin would have gone on the Quebec expedition. An extract from a letter addressed to "Capt. Jas. Chambers, at Ireland's farm, near Cambridge," by John McLellan, and dated "Norwidgewock, 2d Oct., 1775," from the banks of the Kennebec, Maine, says:—"Sir, with my best wishes, I send you this to inform you that it is your indispensable duty to thank God for not permitting the Devil to put it into General Washington's head to send you here." He then gives an account of the wretched country through which they passed, and thinks their sufferings a sufficient punishment for all their sins.

The act of the Congress of 1791, levying duty on spirits distilled in the West, which was intended as an equalization of the imposts on foreign liquors at the seaboard, was resisted with force, and gave rise to the "Whiskey Insurrection." This was a severe test of the strength of the new government, and great apprehension for its safety was everywhere created. Pacific policy failing, prompt and more decisive measures were required to maintain the supremacy of the federal authority; and in 1794, a large military body, in which Col. Chambers commanded a brigade, was marched to the seat of insubordination. Happily, the moral power of this formidable display obviated violent enforcement of order, and a most fearful crisis was thus passed without civil war.

For several years from 1795, General Chambers served in the capacity of Associate Judge of the Franklin County Court of Common Pleas. In 1798, he was appointed Brigadier-General in the Pennsylvania quota of militia, called for by Congress in anticipation of difficulties with

France. The brigade was organized and reported for duty; but its services were not required in the field.

When stationed with the army in New York, he became a member of the Masonic order, and was the founder of the Chambersburg lodge, and its master until his resignation in 1804.

He was a member of the SOCIETY OF THE CINCINNATI, "Instituted by the Officers of the American Army at the Period of its Dissolution, as well to commemorate the great event which gave Independence to North America as for the laudable Purpose of inculcating the Duty of laying down in Peace Arms assumed for public Defence, and of uniting in Acts of brotherly affection and Bonds of perpetual Friendship the Members constituting the same."

Though starting with a liberal estate, his retirement at the close of the war was not marked by exemption from the melancholy fate of shattered constitutions and dilapidated fortunes which awaited the majority of the Revolutionary heroes on their return to private life. He lived in the bland consciousness of having fearlessly striven to promote his country's welfare; and the much-hoped-for end being attained, in peaceful advanced age he encouraged in his children and his neighbors, by precept and example, a sincere love of liberty and direct accountability to God. He died at his residence, at Loudoun Forge, on the evening of the 25th of April, 1805, and was buried with military honors in the last resting-place consecrated by his father.

MEMOIR.

MEMOIR.

CHAPTER I.

Charlotte was the second daughter of General James Chambers and Catherine Hamilton.

The cotemporaries of Charlotte Chambers unite in testifying that she was more than ordinarily lovely in personal and mental endowments. Her figure was above the medium height and combined a pleasing contour of grace and womanly symmetry. A complexion, fair and pure, was increased in effect by a luxuriance of rich brown hair. With nose partaking somewhat of the aquiline type; a mouth of exquisite beauty, and dimpled cheek; and drooping silken lashes, from beneath which dark hazel eyes beamed with health and love—with a manner engaging and conciliatory—to all which the intelligence of a superior and a cultivated mind lent such attraction, and so filled the beau-ideal of maiden charms and feminine perfection, that her name and face were the synonyms of cheerfulness and a ray of sunlight to those, who, once knowing her, valued her society and desired her friendship.

To an amiable disposition were joined gayety of temperament and sparkling wit; while quick perception and ready memory of the best authors, with admirable tact, enabled her to adapt her conversation to the varied tastes of those she met, and to make an impression as creditable to herself as it was acceptable to them.

In that early day, when light literature was neither so plentiful nor so accessible as at the present, and home was looked to more than now for novelty of amusement, she indulged in the prevailing taste for extempore verses, enigmas, and other intellectual fancies to wear away the long winter evenings. In these little accomplishments she was prolific; and to their delicacy and originality the collections of her appreciative acquaintance well attested. Keenly alive to the ludicrous, she blended with it the faculty of narrating anecdote with refreshing vivacity, and of investing her description with irresistible mirth.

To these social attributes were added better and more exalted qualities, which emanate alone from a pure heart and a sincere entertainment of Christian belief. While to the young she was the source of harmless raillery and extravagant fun, she was to the serious and the contemplative, a true companion, whom she would delight by evidences of mature reflection and abundant good sense. In her parental residence her moral nature was nourished. Her mother was notable for domestic virtues and force of character; and her children received the lasting advantages of her careful training.

CATHERINE CHAMBERS was one of those self-sacrificing persons—scarce known beyond the hearth-stone—which the privations of the Revolutionary contest fruitfully developed throughout the American colonies. It is difficult—almost impossible—for us, who repose in the security of moderate government, and the quiet enjoyment of property and existence, to fully comprehend the ever-impending danger of sanguinary conflict, destruction of the products of honest toil, and the ruthless desolation of home and family. In that period, when men felt that the love of country, common justice and the sacred rights of humanity were directing their piteous cries for succor to them individually, and demanding their presence, and even their lives, on the battle-field—then it was, that on woman, in addition to the duties ascribed as peculiarly within her province, devolved the manifold cares of the absent husband or father.

We cannot too fervently hold in grateful remembrance those patriots who gave Freedom the initiative—whose wisdom strengthened by faith in an all-wise Dispenser—whose ardor tempered by prudence, and strong arms backed by unwavering courage—have inured to their descendants in the privileges and the fulness of contentment embraced in the term Republican Liberty.

Our gratitude is not due alone to those intrepid men. They did their part well and nobly. Their cause was just, and God was with them. But they enacted not all the fearful drama; for the Women of the Revolution helped them. Theirs was a silent but not the less potent heroism. Devoid of the pomp and the glory for which most men strive and few obtain, it was akin to the spirit that impelled John Howard, Elizabeth Fry, and the more modern instance, Miss Nightingale, to alleviate the sorrows of suffering mortals, to perform deeds of mercy for the sake of benevolence, and look beyond the grave for the blest reward. Their names cast no imposing shadow of greatness, nor incite a thrill of emotion at thought of battle won and empire gained, but creep tenderly and surely to the inmost recesses of meditative hearts, and there find the meed of praise that is far more expressive, infinitely more welcome, than the noisy acclamation of ten thousand tongues. To attempt a realization of the arduous and lofty responsibilities of the Women of the Revolution, imbues us with enthusiastic admiration, mingled with devout respect for them, for the perils they experienced and the fortitude with which they endured them.

Letters.

TO MRS. CATHERINE CHAMBERS.

WOODBINE,[1] March 5, 1792.

DEAR MAMMA:—

What exquisite joy your letter afforded me! With what pleasure I perused the precious lines portraying the feelings of the heart that dictated them! "Your child of sensibility!"—my dear mother, your child of weakness, I fear, for my eyes flowed; but they were tears of gratitude to Heaven and to thee. May kind Providence long continue to you the blessing of health and peace, and return me to the arms of my indulgent parents!

* * * * *

Having many sources of amusement at home, I declined the invitation to accompany aunt and uncle Ewing to Columbia, but engaged to meet them at Dr. Houston's in the evening. After dinner, Ellen, Miss Sally Dickinson from Wilmington, and myself, sat out by the way of the road. The gently swelling bank of the opposite shore, the numerous little islands interspersed up and down the river, and the distant houses of the Wrights and Bethels, formed a pleasingly picturesque view. We walked with Dr. Houston to the ferry-house, to take a perspective view of Chicus Rock. I wish it were possible for me to describe this stupendous work of nature. On viewing it through the glass, the imagination presents the idea of columns, towers, monuments, obelisks and pyramids, in a confused mass of ruins. A few tall trees crown the summit, waving their tops in the clouds, and seem to look with horror on the gulf below, dreading each blast, lest they should be hurled from their aerial height. We walked into the back parlor, which was profusely decorated with dark-green hemlock. This, with

[1] The letters dated from "Woodbine" were written while on a visit to the family of Gen. Ewing, near Columbia, on the Susquehanna.

coolness, partial gloom, and quiet seclusion, made us almost fancy ourselves in some hermit's moss-grown cave.

We were met there and escorted home by Mr. "Sammy Wright," who, I understand, is the oracle of the neighborhood; and were I to take the words of the people, I should look upon him as a magician, soothsayer, and astrologer! his ways justice, and his words wisdom. So much confidence is placed in his judgment that scarcely any decisive step in this whole neighborhood can be taken until his opinion is known. Indeed, it is considered an unsafe affair to cross the river without him. I wonder what they will do when Sammy Wright dies! Bury him, I suppose, and build a bridge upon his dear remains. Such a basis would support the superstructure to the end of time!

* * * * *

There is so little variety in our mode of life, my dear mother, that I fear my letters will afford you no amusement; but I will write the oftener, and at least prove my solicitude for it.

Your affectionate daughter,

CHARLOTTE CHAMBERS.

TO THE SAME.

WOODBINE, March, 1792.

DEAR MAMMA :—

Aunt has for some time been expecting Miss Mary Mifflin, and yesterday she arrived. She blends in her manner Quaker simplicity with the most refined politeness, and does not affect superiority on account of having passed her life in the metropolis. She is a little near-sighted; but instead of being a defect, it appears in her a grace. Her person is good. Her light auburn hair is covered by a muslin cap and her sleeves just turn the elbow, leaving a pretty arm bare, without even the decoration of a ruffle. She seems cheerful and affectionate. How delightful will my excursions be, accompanied by such a friend! We intend going, as soon as the roads get better, to the Round-Top. And when the wintry winds shall have fled to more northern regions, we are to be wafted by mild breezes on the broad bosom of the Susquehanna, in friend Sammy Wright's batteau, to some of the neighboring islands.

* * * * *

We were admiring the fine landscape from the front door this evening when we observed a boat crossing at the ferry. It was near the middle of the stream, and looked so small I could compare it to nothing but a large aquatic fowl in distress, raising her wings frequently above, and sinking them below the waves. I took the prospect-glass, and was astonished to see a large boat, rowed by six men in white jackets and red caps, filled with gentlemen. I immediately let down the glass lest they should observe me looking at them; but my eye was again presented with the same fluttering little object I had at first beheld. In a short time, the boat landed. The gentlemen were Maj. C., Mr. B. C., Capt. M., and a recruiting officer; so, agreeable raillery, native diffidence, self-importance, and military discipline composed the freight.

In compliance with the invitation of Miss Atlee, who spent the day with us yesterday, we accompanied her to Fairview, the residence of her father, Judge Atlee. It is situated on a high hill, surrounded with shrubbery and lofty trees. * * * We had singing, with the spinnet and flute, during the evening. We staid late. When we returned, the silver moon had reached the zenith, and lent a mellow lustre to every object.

* * * * *

Adieu.

C. C.

TO THE SAME.

WOODBINE, April, 1792.

MY DEAR MOTHER:—

* * Sabbath morning there was Quaker meeting at Columbia, according to custom, and I was impelled by curiosity to attend. My companions no doubt had a motive superior to this. The "Friends" had already assembled, and we took our seats as quietly as possible that we might not disturb their meditations. There were many aged men and women, with their heads covered, and seemingly in profound thought.

I wish this solemn silence was observed in all churches until the audience compose their minds from the hurry of external objects and common conversation, and so prepare themselves for the reception of the grand truths they came to hear. The pause continued unbroken, and I at last began to seek within for thoughts suitable to the occasion. A solemn assembly in the Lord's name, on the Lord's day! I fancied there was in silence, something more eloquent and instructive than in the most elaborate harangue of erudition. The mind learns to rest upon itself. The still, small voice whispers the words of truth, and sits in judgment upon the actions. I considered the peaceful and happy life which is the result of obedience to the precepts of Christianity, and the dreadful situation of the wicked, whose bosoms are like the troubled sea in this world, and their awful state as demoniacs during a never-ending existence!

While thus engaged, one of the old men suddenly arose. He spoke at first with hesitation, as though he was "resisting the Spirit." He had hoped, he said, that his mouth would not have been opened at this time; but he had been in sore travail since he sat down, concerning the dear youth here assembled. He addressed some admonitions to them. In a short time another rose, and spoke a few words on the same subject. Scarcely had he taken his seat, when the first one made a prayer, which closed the meeting. His prayer was the unstudied effusion of a good heart, and had a charm superior to anything that premeditated manner or language could impart.

In conversing with my Quaker friends, I do not defend manners or principles they condemn, nor do I condemn acts which they extol; for I think every sect, with its peculiarities and opinions, possesses goodness in a greater or less degree. Their observance of plain dress may be worthy of praise, and is consistent with the manner they assume. But I think they attach too much importance to trifles when they forbid the use of common forms of salutation. St. Paul was a polite man, agreeably to the etiquette of his day. St. Luke addressed Theophilus as "most excellent." No circumstance, however trivial, relating to the conduct of these two disciples ought to be considered unimportant. They were both men of education, and their actions were never the result of ignorance. Abraham bowed to the sons of Heth. The sons of Israel made obeisance to the governor of Egypt, and St. Paul frequently addressed his audience with, "Sirs." From these and many other instances in the Old and New Testaments, it may be presumed that there is nothing inimical to pure religion in such salutations.

* * * * *

Here I am, writing a long dissertation on Quaker manners, while every other soul in the house is in bed long, long ago; and now I bid you most tenderly good night, my dear mamma. I will go to sleep, and dream about you.

C. C.

TO THE SAME.

WOODBINE, April, 1792.

MY DEAR MOTHER:—

* * What a fascination belongs to flattery! Administered in any shape, it is a staple commodity. It agrees with all constitutions, and thrives in all climates. Some take the raw material in bulk; others require it modified and refined, but still it invariably delights.

* * * * *

* * Our proposed trip to the Round-Top was made yesterday. We left the carriage at the foot of the hill, and pursued the way on foot. The path was steep and covered with stones and bramble. Had we wished to perform penance, a more suitable place could not have been chosen. The day being advanced, we were not allowed time to rest; and almost overcome with fatigue, heat, and thirst, we reached the summit. The ladies had scarcely strength to exclaim, "delightful!" Reaching the top really gave me the most exquisite pleasure; but I beg you will not consider me wanting in appreciation, when I assure you it was more because it afforded a place of rest, than an extensive prospect. I took pains, however, to turn my face toward it as I sat down, which, considering my weariness, was no small proof of good taste.

The river smooth and unbroken, held its course for many miles under my eye, with Donegal and its beautiful neighborhood, dotted with blooming orchards, clumps of forest trees, neat houses, and blue mountains in the distance. Each object was gilded with the setting sun, and the river seemed a stream of molten gold. The mountain on which we stood, was covered with huge rocks, one of which was, by the nervous arms of our guides, raised from its bed where it had reposed since the Deluge. I felt a sensation something like pity when seeing it turn reluctantly from its peaceful rest to the brink of the precipice from which it was to be hurled. Trembling it stood a moment, and in silent eloquence solicited the procrastination of that impulse, which would subject it to such dreadful conflicts—but solicited in vain. The impetus was given; it was agitated, slowly it rolled from side to side, its own weight carrying it onward, and increasing its velocity. Nothing now could impede its progress. Dashing and surging from tree to tree, from rock to rock, it roared terrific horror! The distant hills resounded; Echo heard its wailings, and with a plaintive voice, repeated them through all her gloomy caverns.

Emblem of human life! Reluctant are we rolled from the smooth surface of infancy; we enter with caution on the scenes that present. After some time, self-importance, by magnifying our own powers, makes all objects less formidable in idea. We rush impetuously forward, the sport of contending passions; until astonished, distressed and exhausted, we sink into the vale of death. Scarcely a vestige of our progress remains upon the rugged steep, to transmit to posterity the path we trod, and oblivion soon casts a shade on our names forever! Oh, thou beneficent power, guide and sustain me down some path smoothed by heavenly virtues!

* * * * *

Adieu.

C. C.

TO THE SAME.

WOODBINE, May 4, 1792.

MY DEAR MOTHER :—

* * The first of March I arrived at Woodbine. How dreary was the scene! cold stormy winds, naked hills, muddy roads and pensive hours. Now rosy-footed May, ushered by gentle zephyrs, has clothed the fields in fragrant verdure. The birds warble melodiously through the blooming grove, and the time glides imperceptibly by in cheerful friendship.

* * * * *

At dinner to-day the reading of novels was denounced without mercy, as an unprofitable waste of time and a dangerous amusement for *young ladies!* I became for the occasion a champion in the defence as a means of rational entertainment, and inquired if they had ever known an instance of very great injury resulting from the perusal of fiction? They were obliged to confess they had not.

I am sure history affords many instances of heroic exploits, tender attachments, inviolable friendships, as suddenly commenced, and perhaps as imprudently, as can be found in the field of fiction. If such examples are dangerous, young ladies should not read history, for *truth* must make a greater impression than fable! I would as soon be compelled to subsist on meat, without fruit or vegetables, as to be confined exclusively to sober matter of fact study. In ancient history we read of obscure barbarians rising to fame and glory by force of arms, with the horrid accompaniments of carnage, cruel oppression, massacre, envy, despair, revenge, and death! until we almost contemplate the human species with abhorrence; and can scarcely forbear pronouncing it a race of monsters only tamed by art.

Even in books of travel, we read of arid deserts, burning sands, frozen seas, ferocious animals, poisonous serpents, stinging scorpions; and every variety of human misery. How delightful after those repulsive scenes are the pages of a well written novel or poem; where in the luxuriant images of peaceful valleys, virtuous peasantry, shady groves, roses, myrtle, love and friendship, we become reconciled to life.

I fear, dear mother, you will pronounce my opinions heterodox. *

* * * * *

Your devoted daughter,

C. C.

TO THE SAME.

CHAMBERSBURG, Dec., 1793.

MY DEAR MOTHER:—

Last Saturday we set out in a sleigh amidst a volley of snow balls sent after us by Mr. Dunlop, to visit Dr. and Mrs. Johnson. For several miles, no persons were ever better pleased with themselves or each other. Nature smiled in her white vestments, pure as innocence, and peaceful as ourselves. But alas, a fatal stump! as if to teach us the mutability of human happiness, proved fatal to our progress. In an instant, we were all thrown out and enveloped in snow drifts. One part of the sleigh remained with us; the other, attached to the horses, was proceeding to the Doctor's, as though the Furies were driving. Mr. Colhoon set off as soon as he could disengage himself, to overtake them, and if possible to be in at the "brush!" It would have been a severe brush to us, but for a little one horse sled, that but a few moments before had afforded us a subject for the greatest merriment. After a hearty laugh at our expense, its owners took us in and conveyed us to our place of destination.

Theirs was not the laugh of exulting prosperity over the unfortunate; but the good-natured exuberance of hearts wishing to reconcile us to our situation. Gentle, good souls! when we parted I shook hands with them all round, and thanked them for their facetious benevolence. Interchanges of such kind offices are productive, no doubt, of cordial feeling. As persons living entirely independent of the world become cold and estranged, never experiencing the necessity of receiving such attentions, they are less liable to appreciate them.

* * * * *

Adieu.

C. C.

TO THE SAME.

PHILADELPHIA, Feb. 25, 1795.

MY DEAR MOTHER:—

When I read your compliments to Mrs. Cadwalader, her soul of sensibility was touched, and the tear of affection swelled in her eye.

* * * * *

The morning of the "twenty-second" was ushered in by the discharge of heavy artillery. The whole city was in commotion, making arrangements to demonstrate their attachment to our beloved President. The Masonic, Cincinnati, and military orders united in doing him honor. Happy republic! great and glorious!

* * Mrs. Cadwalader was too much indisposed to attend the ball. Mr. and Mrs. Jackson, with Dr. Spring, called for me in their

coach. Dr. Rodman, master of ceremonies, met us at the door, and conducted us to Mrs. Washington. She half arose as we made our passing compliments. She was dressed in a rich silk, but entirely without ornament, except the animation her amiable heart gives to her countenance. Next her were seated the wives of the foreign ambassadors, glittering from the floor to the summit of their head-dress. One of the ladies wore three large ostrich-feathers. Her brow was encircled by a sparkling fillet of diamonds ; her neck and arms were almost covered with jewels, and two watches were suspended from her girdle, and all reflecting the light from a hundred directions. Such superabundance of ornament struck me as injudicious ; we look too much at the gold and pearls to do justice to the lady. However, it may not be in conformity to their individual taste thus decorating themselves, but to honor the country they represent.

The seats were arranged like those of an amphitheatre, and cords were stretched on each side of the room, about three feet from the floor, to preserve sufficient space for the dancers. We were not long seated when General Washington entered, and bowed to the ladies as he passed round the room. " He comes, he comes, the hero comes !" I involuntarily but softly exclaimed. When he bowed to me, I could scarcely resist the impulse of my heart, that almost burst through my bosom, to meet him.

The dancing soon after commenced. Mr. John Woods, Mr. John Shippen, Lawrence Washington, and Col. Hartley enlivened the time by their attentions, and to them I was much indebted for the pleasure of the evening.

Next morning I received an invitation by my father from Mrs. Washington to visit her, and Col. Hartley politely offered to accompany me to the next drawing-room levee.

* * * * *

On this evening my dress was white brocade silk, trimmed with silver, and white silk, high-heeled shoes, embroidered with silver, and a light blue sash, with silver cord and tassel tied at the left side. My watch was suspended at the right, and my hair was in its natural curls. Surmounting all was a small white hat and white ostrich-feather, confined by brilliant band and buckle. Punctual to the moment, Col.

Hartley, in his chariot, arrived. He brought with him Dr. Price, from England, who has sought America as an asylum, having given some political umbrage to his own government.

The hall, stairs, and drawing-room of the President's house were well lighted by lamps and chandeliers. Mrs. Washington, with Mrs. Knox, sat near the fire-place. Other ladies were seated on sofas, and gentlemen stood in the centre of the room conversing. On our approach, Mrs. Washington arose and made a courtesy—the gentlemen bowed most profoundly—and I calculated my declension to her own with critical exactness.

The President soon after, with that benignity peculiarly his own, advanced, and I arose to receive and return his compliments with the respect and love my heart dictated. He seated himself beside me, and inquired for my father, a severe cold having detained him at home.

* * * * *

C. C.

TO THE SAME.

PHILADELPHIA, March 11, 1795.

MY DEAR MOTHER:—

I have but few moments to spare. Engagements abroad and company at home occupy my time; and such is the variety of Philadelphia, every day brings some new pursuit, and is passed in the perpetual rotation of what is termed pleasure. Everywhere I experience those attentions which render my excursions from the city, and my visits in it, invariably pleasing.

In a previous letter, I wrote of being at the President's, and my admiration of Mrs. Washington. Yesterday, Col. Proctor informed me that her carriage was at the door, and a servant inquiring for me. * * After the usual compliments and some conversation, she gave me a pressing invitation to spend the day with her; and so perfectly friendly were her manners, I found myself irresistibly attached to her. On taking leave, she observed a portrait of the President hanging over the fire-place, and said "She had never seen a correct likeness of General

Washington. The only merit the numerous portraits of him possessed was their resemblance to each other."

We dined yesterday at Mr. John Nicholson's. There was a large party. * * We spent the evening at Mrs. Madison's, and Mr. and Mrs. J. have invited a party to dine at Belle Air to-morrow. Miss Binney and myself, while walking this afternoon with Augustus Muhlenburg and Septimus Claypoole, met Gen. Scott, of Kentucky. He said he had just called on us to propose a party to Gray's Gardens. He has an extensive acquaintance, great originality, and is constantly endeavoring to vary and increase our amusements. * * * * *

I must finish this letter to-morrow, as the carriage has arrived, and I am engaged to accompany Dr. Bedford, Gen. and Mrs. Neville, and my father to the theatre.

* * * * *

Adieu, devotedly,

C. C.

CHAPTER II.

In 1787, Israel Ludlow, of New Jersey, who was at that time twenty-three or twenty-four years of age, received the following letter from the Surveyor-General and Geographer to the United States:—

To Israel Ludlow, Esq.—

Dear Sir: I inclose to you an ordinance of Congress of the 20th inst., by which you will observe they have agreed to the sale of a large tract of land, which the New Jersey Society have contracted to purchase. As it will be necessary to survey the boundary of this tract with all convenient speed, that the United States may receive the payment for the same, I propose to appoint you for that purpose, being assured of your abilities, diligence, and integrity. I hope you will accept it, and desire that you will furnish me with an estimate of the expense, and inform me what monies will be necessary to advance to you to enable you to execute the same.

I am, dear sir,
Yours,
Tho. Hutchins,
Surveyor-General, U. S.

He accepted the appointment, and received with his instructions, an order on the frontier posts for a sufficient escort to enable him to prosecute the surveys. The reply below to his application, shows the extreme weakness of the military force then in the Northwest Territory, and the dangerous nature of the duty upon which he was employed. Gen. Harmar was the commanding officer in the valley of the Ohio, and Fort Harmar stood at the mouth of the Muskingum.

FORT HARMAR, Aug. 28, 1788.

MR. ISRAEL LUDLOW :—

SIR : The letter you delivered me from the War Office, informs me that you have been appointed to survey the exterior lines of the purchase made by Cutler and Sargent, and directs me to furnish adequate guards for your protection.

I am sorry that it is out of my power to comply with the said directions, for these reasons, viz : In the first place, this garrison is daily becoming too weak, as the men's time is expiring. In the next, if the guards could be furnished, as the general treaty is about to take place, and a large number of the Indians are hunting in the very country you would be going through, I think it imprudent that you should undertake the business at this season, until the result of the treaty is known.

I am, sir,

Your very humble servant,

JOS. HARMAR.

In the winter of 1789 he became associated with Matthias Denman and Robert Patterson in the proprietorship of the future Cincinnati to the extent of one-third interest.

Such have been the claims of various individuals to the naming of this place, and so diverse the testimony in substantiation thereof, that it is deemed but simple justice to copy from "Burnet's Notes on the Northwestern Territory," a succinct and exceedingly interesting account, which sets forth Mr. Ludlow's connection with Cincinnati, and certainly creates the impression that through him our city gained its present noble and dignified name:—

"Matthias Denman of Springfield, New Jersey, had purchased the fraction of land on the bank of the Ohio, and the entire section adjoining it on the north, which on the survey of Symmes' grant should be found to lie opposite the mouth of Licking River. In the summer of 1788 he came out to the West to see the lands he had purchased, and to examine the country. On his return to Limestone[1] he met, among others, Col. R. Patterson, of Lexington, Kentucky, and a surveyor named Filson. Denman communicated to them the intention of laying out a town on his land opposite Licking; and after some conversation, agreed to take them in as partners, each paying a third of the purchase money, and on the farther condition that Col. Patterson should exert his influence to obtain settlers, and that Filson in the ensuing spring, should survey the town, stake off the lots and superintend the sale. They also agreed upon the plan of the town, and to call it Losantiville; a compound word intended to express 'the city opposite the mouth of Licking.'

"This being done, Patterson and Filson with a party of settlers proceeded to the ground, where they arrived late in December. In the course of the winter, before any attempts had been made to lay out the town, Filson went on an exploring expedition with Judge Symmes and others who had it in contemplation to become purchasers and settle in the country.

"After the party had proceeded some distance in the wilderness, Filson left them for the purpose of returning to the settlements on the Ohio, and in that attempt he was murdered by the Indians. This terminated his contract with Denman, as no part of the consideration had been paid, and his personal services in surveying the town and superintending the sale had become impracticable.

"Mr. Denman being yet at Limestone, entered into another contract with Col. Patterson and Israel Ludlow, by which Ludlow was to perform

[1] Now Maysville, Ky.

the same services as were to have been rendered by the unfortunate Filson, had he lived to execute his contract. A new plan of a town was made, differing in many respects from the former, particularly as to the public square, the commons, and the names of the streets. The whimsical name which had been adopted for the town to be laid out under the first contract, was repudiated, and Cincinnati selected as the name of the town to be laid out under the new contract. Late in the succeeding fall (1789) Col. Ludlow commenced a survey of the town, which has since become the 'Queen City of the West.'"

Five miles from Cincinnati in the valley of Mill Creek, Mr. Ludlow established a large farm. It included what is now the Spring Grove Cemetery and parts of the attractive suburb of Clifton, and the town of Cumminsville. A dense forest covered the tract, but soon gave place to cultivated fields. The orchards, the garden, and other improvements were projected on a liberal scale, and in accordance with the best taste of those days.

A block house was the first tenement erected here, and LUDLOW STATION was known as the nearest secure military post beyond Fort Washington.[1] The Station was the resort of the Indians, where they were always sure of food and the pipe. Scarcely ever was the yard or the lawn in front, seen without the thin blue curl of the smoke from their lodge fires. They were not then restrained by treaty, and would kill and rob those they could catch in the vicinity of the fords or other convenient lurking places. A letter of Mrs. Ludlow says:—

[1] This was near the north line of the town plat of Cincinnati.

Shortly after we arrived in Cincinnati, Mr. Ludlow was commissioned to fix the boundary line between the United States and the Indians, agreeably to the treaty of Greenville made by Gen. Wayne in 1795. I still recollect with pain my regret for the sufferings endured by Mr. L., and my gloomy apprehensions for his safety.

With Denman and Patterson as equal proprietors, he laid out in 1788 the city of Cincinnati.[1] In December, 1794, he surveyed the plat of a town adjacent to Fort Hamilton—hence the name—and was sole owner. In November, 1795, in conjunction with Gens. St. Clair, Dayton and Wilkinson, he founded the town of Dayton.

In 1790 were created White's, Covolt's, and Ludlow stations. Gen. Harmar placed soldiers for defence at these forts, and persons who ventured beyond sight of them, often fell victims to savage ferocity. In 1791, Gen. St. Clair's army encamped at Ludlow Station, on the ground where the orchard now is. On the 17th of September, he proceeded to the Great Miami, and erected Forts Hamilton and Jefferson, and on the 4th November was fought the bloody and unfortunate battle called "St. Clair's Defeat." Col. Wilkinson and Maj. John S. Gano, with a party of regulars and militia, repaired to the field of battle, and performed the humane and melancholy duty of burying the dead.

At this period, when attending religious or other meetings, the men were obliged to take with them their firearms for protection. In 1793, Gen. Wayne succeeded St. Clair, and prosecuted the war until its termination in 1795. Emigration then again commenced, and new towns and farms spread through the yielding forest.

When I arrived, in Feb. 1797, Cincinnati was a village of wooden buildings, with a garrison of soldiers. The society consisted of a small number of ladies, united by the most perfect good-will and desire for mutual happiness. The gentlemen were social and intelligent. Among those who have become identified with its early history, I mention, with almost fraternal regard, Judge McMillan, Col. Wallace, Judge Burnet, Rev. O. M. Spencer, Gen. Gano, Gen. Findlay, Gen. Harrison, Gen. St. Clair, Gov. Sargent, Geo. Burnet, Esq., Dr. Allison, Dr. Selmon, Jesse Hunt, Esq., and Maj. Ziegler.

[1] His camp was near the intersection of Main and Front Sts.

Some of these are gone; but let their cotemporaries who remain, look forward to regions of immortality where we shall meet under the influences of a more perfect economy, and where changes shall be no more.

The surveys (prescribed by the instructions of Hutchins in 1787) were prosecuted, notwithstanding the hostility of the savages and the deficiency of escort, but with the inevitable delay attending the movements of small parties where precaution from danger so materially engrossed the attention. The letter here quoted to Gen. Hamilton explains the cause of the slow progress of the survey, and presents in a striking manner, scenes of pioneer exposure and hardship.

PHILADELPHIA, May 5, 1792.

SIR:—

The unexpected delays that have attended my executing the surveys of the Ohio and Miami Companies, together with your letters, which I have received from time to time, urging my speedy exertions to effect the business, induces me to explain to you the cause of the delay.

In Nov., 1790, I was honored with your letter of instruction at this place. I proceeded immediately to Fort Harmar, being possessed of Gen. Knox's letter, or order to the Commandant for an escort. On my way, at Fort Pitt, I saw Maj. Doughty, who, after becoming acquainted with my business, informed me that there was no doubt but an escort would be furnished on my arrival at Fort Harmar, upon which I supplied myself with chain-carriers and other hands necessary, pack-horses, corn, provision, and camp equipage for the approaching cold season.

On my arrival at Fort Harmar, I found no escort could be obtained. Maj. Zeigler,[1] who commanded, gave me his answer in writing, which

[1] There is a confusion of names here, as the reply to the application was from Gen. Harmar.

was that he did not consider the troops then under his command, more than sufficient to guard the settlement of Marietta, the Indians having shortly before that, defeated and broken up one of their frontier stations. Of course, he could not comply with the order of Gen. Knox and my request (a copy of that letter I inclosed to you). Upon that information, from necessity I gave up the pursuit at that time, and proceeded to Fort Washington, supposing I could execute the Miami survey.

Discharging my hired men and pack-horses, I applied to Gen. Harmar, who then commanded, for protection while surveying the Miami tract. He informed me he did not consider his whole command a sufficient escort for my purpose (a copy of his answer I forwarded to you). On the arrival of Gen. St. Clair, in May following, I made an official application for fifteen men or more, should it be convenient, to accompany me as an escort while surveying the Miami and Ohio tracts. He assured me that he considered the execution of this survey a matter of the highest interest and importance to the United States, and that he would make every effort to assist me with a sufficient guard, but that it was then impracticable (his letter I will forward to you). Thus, the business was again put off until the 20th of October following, when I was favored with the services of fifteen men, commanded by a serjeant, with whom I proceeded to execute the Ohio Co.'s survey. I succeeded, and returned to Fort Washington, but with the loss of six of the escort, and leaving in the woods all my pack-horses and their equipage, and being obliged to make a raft of logs to descend the Ohio as far as Limestone, from opposite the mouth of the Great Sandy river.

On my arrival at Fort Washington, I again applied for protection to proceed in the Miami survey. That assistance was refused by Maj. Zeigler, who then commanded (his letter I will produce). My reputation, as well as the public good, being in some measure affected by the delay of the business, I was constrained to have recourse to an effort which my instruction did not advise, viz. : to attempt making the survey by the aid of three active woodsmen, to assist as spies, and give notice of any approaching danger. My attempts proved unsuccessful. After extending the western boundary more than one hundred miles up the Miami river, the deep snows and cold weather rendered our situation too distressing, by reason of my men having their feet frozen, and unfit to furnish game for supplies. In consequence, we returned to Fort Washington. The cold weather abating, I made another attempt, extending the east boundary as far as the line intersected the Little Miami river, where we discovered signs of the near approach of Indians, and, having but three armed men in company, induced me to return again to Fort Washington, which I found commanded by Gen. Wilkinson, to whom I applied for an escort, which was denied me (his letter I have the honor to inclose to you with the others).

I now have the satisfaction to present to you the whole of the survey of the Ohio, and part of the Miami, purchases, executed agreeably to instructions. Any further information that may be required respecting the causes of delay of the above business, I presume may be had from Gens. St. Clair and Harmar, who are now here present.

I am, sir, yours respectfully,

ISRAEL LUDLOW.

HON. ALEX. HAMILTON,
Sec. of the Treasury.

CHAPTER III.

During the spring of 1796, Mr. Ludlow tarried at Loudoun, near Chambersburg, on his route to Philadelphia. It may readily be inferred how much his intelligent and accurate information of the teeming West recommended him to the polite hospitality of Gen. Chambers, and how favorably his adventurous life and manly bearing intuitively won the regard of the daughter.

In the succeeding November, the marriage of Charlotte Chambers and Israel Ludlow took place; and she who had been reared in the enjoyments of an elegant home, in the midst of a long-established community, and was the object of the fondest maternal regard; without repining, left all these to brave the discomforts and the hazards of the emigration to Ohio, and to cheerfully submit to the numberless inconveniences of a residence in a newly located western town.

We can but ill imagine now, the difficulties attendant upon such a journey on horseback at that time. The accommodations were poor, and of the most wretched description; and at night, the short distance compassed since the gray dawn by the weary traveller, through the steep and stony passes of the Alleghanies, rendered the prospect of reaching the ultimate destination forlorn indeed.

TO MRS. CHAMBERS.

RED-STONE OLD-FORT, Dec. 19, 1796.

MY DEAR MOTHER:—

We are now at Col. Shreve's, and if they were not one of the kindest families in the world, we should fall into a state of torpor. We seem to live mainly for the purpose of eating and sleeping. "Now," said our fellow guest, Capt. Brown, while at dinner, "we have nothing more to do to-day, but eat our supper, say our prayers, and go to bed!"

We shall descend to Pittsburg in a boat.[1] Business will detain us a few days, and then we take our departure for Cincinnati. I have had perfect health since I left home, and I pray for fortitude and resignation to strengthen me in whatever trials I may encounter. * * * But at present I dare not think of home. The image of beloved friends who are so far distant, and who are so necessary to my happiness, has too powerful an influence on my heart. Absence and time eradicate slight attachments, but increase and refine the higher and more noble.

* * * * *

Adieu, my dear mother, and be assured that time, distance, and absence, by teaching me your value, will only increase my affection for you.

CHARLOTTE C. LUDLOW.

[1] The boats in that early day were long, narrow and flat-bottomed (commonly called scows), propelled by the force of the river current, aided by great sweep-oars balanced on a wooden pivot, and worked by two or more men. These scows were of the most temporary construction, and built of pine or other light wood, which could serve as building material at the end of the journey.

TO THE SAME.

MARIETTA, Feb. 13, 1797.

MY DEAR MOTHER:—

You must excuse my long silence, which has not proceeded from inattention, but from the want of an opportunity of conveying a letter. When I wrote to you last, our situation resembled the fabled misery of Tantalus, as the society which Pittsburg afforded was beyond our reach. The weather became so inclement, we were precluded from going there by land, and every few days wrought some flattering change in the prospect, that we should soon be able to go by water. But nine long weeks elapsed before we embarked on the Monongahela. The second morning after leaving, we breakfasted in Pittsburg, and had the pleasure of experiencing from its inhabitants, such attentions as convinced us they were as interesting and social as our anticipations had pictured them. We passed two days there; and our time was so completely occupied, it was in vain to attempt snatching a moment to write.

Col. Ludlow has many friends in this place. We dined yesterday at Gen. Putnam's, and to-night a ball is given on our account. To-morrow we leave Marietta for Cincinnati, and will carry with us a grateful sense of the kindness we have met with here.

* * * * *

I assure you, my dear mother, the happiness I had anticipated in wedded life has been more than realized. I was so fearful of the bitterness of disappointment consequent on anticipating too much perfection in the human character, that I approached the subject with subdued and moderate calculations; but my husband's generous affection and admirable character have secured my gratitude and love.

Adieu.

C. L.

TO THE SAME.

CINCINNATI, April, 1797.

MY DEAR MOTHER :—

* * Major Zeigler said to me on his first visit, "Our ladies are not gay; but they are extremely affectionate, one to another." I believe he spoke truth. Perfect harmony and good-will appear to exist in all their intercourse, and I feel already attached to them.

Mrs. John Cleves Symmes, lately Miss Livingston, of New York, and Mrs. W. H. Harrison, daughter of Judge J. C. Symmes, visited me in company. I was pleased with both ladies. Mrs. Symmes is a fine-looking woman, with much dignity of manner, and is said to possess superior mental abilities. Mrs. Harrison is delicate in her person, and her manners indicate sweetness of disposition and goodness of heart. One seems to demand our admiration, and the other to solicit our affection.

* * * * *

Fort Washington is situated on the brow of the first hill south of Fourth Street and east of Broadway, and commands a fine view of the town. Licking river flows in immediately opposite, and its beautiful valley is limited by undulating hills.

* * * * *

C. L.

TO THE SAME.

CINCINNATI, May 2, 1797.

MY DEAR MOTHER :—

The hours move with insupportable dulness. Col. Ludlow's absence this time will be short, but there will succeed one of four months. May Heaven sustain him, and grant me fortitude so that my useless regrets may not render the separation unnecessarily painful to him! He is appointed to run the line between the United States and the Indian Territory. He is to meet the chiefs of the various tribes. Many gentlemen join the party from motives of speculation and curiosity, and they will have an escort of soldiers.

* * * * *

My husband is active from principle, as well as constitutionally. In his view, indolence and vice are synonymous. As motives to reconcile me to our frequent separation, he says, "Have we not, my dear Charlotte, many happy years to spend together? Let us not render them gloomy by repinings. The absence of a few months may procure advantages to the country and to ourselves that, if now neglected, no succeeding period can retrieve."

* * * * *

I often transport myself in fancy to you, and the lovely garden where I passed so many hours of exquisite pleasure. The greenbrier, the hawthorn, the honeysuckle, the bank of grape-vine, but more than all, the silent enchantment of the sheltered summer-house! There I first heard the avowed preference of my beloved Ludlow. The time, the fragrance that breathed from all around, and the seclusion, banished the idea from our minds that we were strangers! He expressed his admiration of the place; the transition to admiration of one who listened with such pleased attention was natural. Never did I visit that spot afterwards without a recurrence of the sentiments forever associated with it. They overcome me even now when I visit it in imagination!

It gives me pleasure to know that my dear mother values those places I took so much delight in improving, and that we loved them alike, and that our tastes were assimilated. * * When we improve our farm, I will endeavor to create there a resemblance to the beauties of Loudoun.

Thank my dear father for his expressions of kindness. The idea of taking me from friends so tenderly loved, where I was cherished with such fondness, and yet compelled to leave me so much alone, gives pain to my beloved husband. But, believe me, not one sigh of regret that I have forsaken all for him ever disturbs my peace.

* * * * *

C. L.

LUDLOW STATION, Dec.

JOURNAL.—As many incidents in a life of tranquillity soon pass to oblivion, my sweet friend, Sally Brown, who is spending the winter with me, insists that I shall note at the close of each day, or other moments of leisure, during my husband's absence, the various occurrences that transpire, that they may assist our memory when taking a retrospective survey of time, with its providences, during this monotonous, uneventful season. Supported hitherto in mercy, we trust for a continuation of favor. Blessed with health and every comfort, our frequent separation is the only cause of sorrow.

The tenth of Nov., 1796, we were united, Mr. Ludlow being in my opinion the perfection of manly loveliness. Dr. King performed the marriage ceremony. A few hours after, I said to the Doctor, "When my sister Bella married, you neglected to enforce a promise of obedience; but from Mr. Dunlop you exacted one of indulgence. To-day you have bound me to obey and submit, and Mr. Ludlow has only received an injunction to love and protect. Will you explain this inconsistency?" "There is no inconsistency, my dear daughter," he answered; "on these occasions, I always study character."

On the twentieth day of the same month we bade adieu to our friends, and set out for the Western Territory. After a tedious journey over the mountains, we reached the Monongahela river, and descended in a small boat to the vicinity of Pittsburg. Here, we embarked on the waters of the beautiful Ohio. Although destitute of verdure, the varied landscape presented interesting scenery. High banks, covered with stately forests, appeared; then a tributary stream, emptying its accumulated flood. The next moment, low sloping ground met the eye, with an extended river prospect, an island, or in the more distant view, the commencement of a new settlement, where but a short time before, the soil was impressed by no foot save of the wild beast or the wandering Indian.

TO MR. LUDLOW.

CINCINNATI, May, 1797.

MY DEAR LUDLOW :—

* * I have been informed that when the Shawnees met, they appointed a chief almost unknown to attend you; and if your present engagements could have been postponed until October, the principal men of the different tribes would have accompanied you. This has renewed doubts which you had almost succeeded in dissipating. I fear little reliance can be placed in their good faith, from such an appointment, and less on the influence or power of an inferior chief to protect you should difficulty or danger occur. How earnestly I wish for your return! Let no motive, my love, induce you to encounter personal hazard, nor admit any circumstance having an appearance of hostility to pass unnoticed. Suffer not the idea of safety to relax for one moment the unremitting watchfulness and order that excludes the possibility of surprise. But be careful to conceal any distrust you might have cause to entertain, which would only alienate their friendship, and produce those results you wish to avoid. I rely as much on your coolness and prudence, as on your inflexible courage. I know your firmness and undeviating rectitude, and I have no fear of your acting rashly. But still I know the difficulty of guarding against savage treachery.

* * * * *

I humbly pray Heaven to grant you success, and make me happy by your return!

C. L.

TO THE SAME.

CINCINNATI, 1797.

MY DEAR LUDLOW :—

* * The anxiety I experience on your account can admit of no mitigation, until I receive from your own hand an assurance of your safety. The idea that I have beheld you perhaps for the last time, tortures me and defies all exertion to overcome it.

It is the opinion of Gen. Wilkinson, that the business cannot proceed in safety, as the Indians are not disposed to allow its continuance. Of what importance would an imaginary line be to savages determined to know no boundary? Heaven alone can foresee what consequences might ensue from the smallest degree of rashness on your part. What a desert would this world be to me, should you fall by their hands!

I cannot but contrast the period of unmingled felicity in which I experienced the unremitting care, and affectionate attentions of a husband so beloved as you, with the dreary blank of my present existence. The reverse would be sufficiently sad, had I no apprehensions in regard to your safety. You entreat me to be *happy!* The expectation of happiness in your absence is an illusion. Your precious letter, I have read again and again. But I shall spare you the expressions of my anxiety.

* * * * *

I entreat that no uneasiness on my account may disturb you, and the thoughts of your love and your return, shall give cheerfulness and peace to my bosom. Rest assured, my beloved, let your determination to return be as it may, that decision I shall consider right.

May that gracious and almighty power, which has hitherto protected you in times of danger, govern your resolves!

Adieu,

C. L.

TO MRS. S. B. DUNLOP.

CINCINNATI, July 1, 1797.

DEAR SISTER BELLA:—

During my distress on learning of your dangerous illness, Col. Ludlow was compelled to leave home. Horrible reports respecting Indian aggression were daily gaining currency. I resisted his intention of trusting to their fidelity, with all the arguments that reason and affection could suggest—but reasoned in vain. Tears and entreaties were equally unavailing. Three times he left me to mount his horse, and as often returned, unable to leave me in my wretchedness. He at length succeeded in reviving the sunshine of hope upon the anticipation of our future meeting; and partially recalled that fortitude so necessary to my support.

* * * * *

I can unbosom my heart to you, my dear sister, and speak of its deprivations and emotions with perfect confidence in your sympathy. Sometimes, indeed, the thought of living, deprived of the society of those I fervently love, terminates in a burst of irrepressible tears. But at other times when I regain strength, to calmly contemplate the blessings which remain, I find I have greatly overlooked my mercies; and as my husband has heretofore been protected from savage ferocity, it would be sinful to doubt the same providential goodness for the future. I shall seek for consolation in that ever present, overruling power, in which I have hitherto had my confidence.

* * * * *

Adieu. C. L.

TO GENERAL CHAMBERS.

CINCINNATI, July 7, 1797.

MY DEAR FATHER:—

I wish you would conclude seriously on making us a visit. I think you would be almost willing to abandon the rough lands of Franklin County for this luxuriant country, where even the hills are covered with a deep soil, and the ploughshare turns the furrows, with the cheering prospect of obtaining a hundred bushels of corn to the acre.

Our farm affords advantages that will give me pleasure to cultivate to a high degree of rural elegance. The house is large and commodious for this new country. It is situated on an eminence, and at the base of the hill flows a pellucid stream of never-failing water. From the elevation of the fountain, I entertain the hope that we will be enabled to conduct it through the garden we are planning on the declivity. The buildings are progressing, and we think they will soon be habitable. I shall certainly regret leaving Cincinnati, but the thought of embellishing a place that is to be our residence for life, the home of my family, and where I expect to repose in death, is an inducement more than adequate to every other consideration.

The arrival of Gen. Wilkinson has imparted an air of gayety to the town, and groups of officers in uniform, give a show of fête. There has been a succession of dinners and evening parties. The General's appearance and manner are much in his favor, and he is very popular; and was received with the customary military honors.

* * * * *

Our brilliant Fourth of July celebration was terminated by a sad accident. The party opposed to the Governor, glowing with all the heroism of "Seventy-Six," mounted a blunderbuss on the bank of the river, and with a few hearts of steel made its shores resound, rivalling in their imagination the ordnance of the garrison! Delighted with their success, the load was increased in proportion to their enthusiasm; and when the "Western Territory" was toasted, the gun summoned every power within it, carried its thunder through the Kentucky hills, and burst in pieces! Major Zeigler, on taking a view of the field, reports as follows:—

Wounded,	Four men.
Killed,	One gun!

* * * * *

C. L.

TO MRS. JOHNSON.

LUDLOW STATION, Sep. 8, 1798.

DEAR MRS. JOHNSON:—

Your ladyship's silence I find unconquerable. I had hopes of starving you out; but, alas, I have been compelled to capitulate on your own terms! I had determined to stand on points, and make a pretext of etiquette, engagements, and many other equally grave considerations. But affection has this moment vanquished all those mighty impediments, and I hope you will feel duly complimented by my want of perseverance.

* * * * *

I am grateful for the solicitude expressed by my friends for my "insulated situation." But I assure you and them, every wish of my heart is so entirely filled, every dream of my earliest fancy so completely realized, that my soul kindles with adoration to the great Disposer of my destiny.

* * * * *

* * I hope in a year or two to visit Pennsylvania, and am prepared to witness surprising revolutions. Beaux will be lost in husbands, belles in matrons, and some will have passed from the theatre of life. But the mutability of earthly scenes shall never obliterate from my bosom the steadfast affection with which you ever have been regarded by your far distant friend.

C. L.

Journal.—Tuesday. I sat late last night, being alone, reading Miller's natural history of mountains, and the source and formation of rivers. What an imperfect idea must we have, helpless and insignificant as we are, of that power which called worlds to life, and filled them with objects for wonder and admiration, and at whose word on the great day, the dead are to be raised to hear the final judgment! In view of this sublime occasion, what manner of person should we be in all holy conversation and godliness? Oh, may we be enabled to build upon that foundation where nothing can alarm during the coming desolation of all matter!

* * * * *

How easy the transition from nature to grace! and I turned with pleasure to the latter subject, so admirably treated by the commanding mind of Dr. Witherspoon in his treatise on Regeneration, and which is conducted with such profound reasoning, such unaffected zeal.

Evening.—The engagements of the day being over, my two children asleep by a bright fire in my own comfortable room, I finished Dr. Witherspoon's treatise.

> "Oh, lost to virtue, lost to manly thought,
> Lost to the noblest sallies of the soul,
> Who think it solitude to be alone!"

Almighty Father, merciful, long suffering, and abundant in goodness! In Thee, O glorious Creator! do we live, move, and have our being.

May we in faithfulness and sincerity serve Thee, and devote ourselves to Thy glory. Grant that my parents, my sisters, brother and friends may all be born of God. Though forests and mountains now intervene, may we all meet to celebrate Thy praise beyond the everlasting hills.

* * * * *

Saturday Evening, Dec. * On visiting Cincinnati to-day, I found our agreeable acquaintance, Mrs. K., indisposed. Far from her country and relatives, ill and solitary, without the attention of her husband, she excited the kindest sympathy. She promised to make us a visit. Come, my charming friend, and while your gayety gilds the fleeting moments of a winter evening, let me in friendship lead your mind to enjoyments more worthy of its ambition. * * *

Monday Morning.—Rapidly the moments hurry on! The few last years appear as yesterday. Innumerable mercies have we experienced unacknowledged. No painful incident marks the routine; but blessed with unanimity of opinion, health, and plenty, our hearts should be deeply impressed with gratitude to the bountiful bestower—

> "Heaven's favors here are trials, not rewards,
> A call to duty, not discharge from care,
> And should alarm us full as much as woe,
> And wake us to their cause and consequence."

Night.—I rode over to see poor Mrs. A., whom I found very sick. I remained with her until nearly nine o'clock, and returned alone on my faithful horse, Prince. Snow covered the ground; the moon was almost set, and nature was still. Abundant cause have I for adoration and praise. A few months since, I too was afflicted with severe illness, and have been raised and strengthened, I trust, for future usefulness.

Our conversation was on prayer. Mrs. A. said she could not pray audibly, but "fervently in the spirit." I told her to solicit with the voice, for we are encouraged to believe, by many instances recorded in the Scriptures, that audible prayer was frequently successful. The blind man who cried aloud, "Jesus, thou son of David, have mercy on me!" affords an instance of successful loud importunity.

But still, as the command of Christ was to "enter into thy closet and pray secretly," from the observation of men, and as the compassionate Redeemer has promised always to be ready and willing to hear the fervent prayer of faith, He undoubtedly regards the sincerity of heart with which it is uttered, whether it be breathed in silence or cried aloud.

JAN. 12, 1802.—Mr. Ludlow has been absent a month. The weather is intensely cold, with sleet and snow. He being a degree further north, must experience a colder atmosphere. May Heaven protect him! * *

JAN. 20.—The sun arose with unusual splendor, and continued its brilliancy throughout the day. It was productive of the most happy effects. Had the gloom lasted much longer, the evil consequences would have been great, for the electric fluid of cheerfulness, so ingeniously described by Brydone, would have entirely evaporated. The children were fretful, the servants surly and impatient, and nervous irritability was threatening all. But the sunshine has dissipated unpleasant feelings, and contentment is restored, although I feel increased anxiety on Mr. Ludlow's account. May confidence in a protecting Providence allay my fears!

* * * * *

EVENING.—This morning I thought of Solomon's advice, "Look well to thy flocks," and impressed with the obligation of duty in my husband's absence, I summoned my good Prince, and rode to the distant meadows, and saw the men distribute bountifully to the cattle. I then proceeded to visit our sick neighbors. Mrs. W. was apparently very low, but composed. Her cabin exhibited many a crack to admit the "bitter blast." On my return, I sent a man to repair them, and with other things contributed to make the family more comfortable.

* * * * *

Comparison with wretchedness should increase our gratitude. I am by nature equally unworthy, and by practice more so, yet great the contrast in our situations. She wants, and I have to spare; and I must not withhold a helping hand. Should I, who need so much forgiveness, deny assistance to a fellow traveller?

TO BENJAMIN CHAMBERS.

LUDLOW STATION, March.

DEAR BROTHER :—

I am happy to learn of your marriage. I was apprehensive that your extreme sensitiveness and diffidence were illy calculated to succeed with each other. But you have surmounted these little obstacles, and now the same assiduity continued, will suppress all others. You cannot form a better criterion for future mutual conduct than your present feelings. That forbearance, that accommodation to procure each other happiness, and that attention to the smallest things that may be supposed to produce the pleasure you now experience, will infallibly secure its continuance. Frequently, from the neglect of things in themselves of no importance, difficulties arise in married life which a little good-nature and a little common sense might have prevented. If the indulgence of a few whims will constitute the smallest gratification, it is unwise not to comply with them. Time refines and exalts the virtues of the soul; and that union which has those for the basis, will never know a decrease of affection.

We anticipate much pleasure in your society. R. is too liberal to suppose that happiness has any peculiar locality; and those friends who bind us to our favorite spot, are not even there always with us, nor do we annex the idea of misery to their absence from it.

* * * * *

The distance that separates us excludes not the pleasure of hearing from you frequently. We participate in idea, in all the festivity of the wedding. Bella wrote us the particulars, and perhaps—nay, positively—my view of it is now as vivid as hers. Instead of repining at our absence, we transport ourselves to you, and partake of all the joys of the occasion. Happy ingredient in the human constitution! Many tedious moments have we beguiled of their lassitude and converted into real pleasure by its benign influence.

C. L.

CHAPTER IV.

About this period, Mrs. Ludlow was seized with a dangerous and protracted illness, of the nature of which we are not now aware. During this, her mind was filled with the deepest anguish for the salvation of her soul. Her wounded spirit, day after day, sought relief in reading the Scriptures, and in conversation with pious friends. Again and again, in the early morning, at noon, and in the wakeful hours of the long weary night, she humbly addressed the throne of grace. But it was in the bitterness of despair, for there was not the sweet return for which her desponding intuitions yearned.

No light, no hope visited her stricken heart, or relieved her from the terrors of the anticipated punishment of an offended God. She saw him only in his attributes of majesty and justice, and feared that his face was forever averted from her. Though pure and innocent had been her life, she felt herself irretrievably lost in the withdrawal of his presence.

One night the family were summoned to the sick room. Parched with fever and suffering with an increase of alarming symptoms, her weeping friends supposed her dying.

At this crisis, her faithful physician, Dr. Allison, entered the room. He had been aroused from sleep by an impression of her sudden danger, and was irresistibly impelled at this gloomy hour to leave his bed, and ride those five miles in the dark night over rough roads. By his admirable skill, and with the blessing of Heaven, the dread hand of death was happily arrested.

Her heart overflowed in thankfulness for this new, and (by her considered) undeserved mercy; and from that time she lived to unceasingly praise the Redeemer's name, and to make His cause her principal duty. "Let us live to His glory, the world is nothing to me," was her worthy and well-followed maxim.

TO MRS. CHAMBERS.

LUDLOW STATION.

MY DEAR MOTHER:—

Although my nerves are weak and trembling, I will try to give you the history of my illness and recovery. * * * * *

* * Dr. Allison and Dr. Selmon, unwearied in kindness, left me but seldom, and my husband was scarcely absent a moment. As my fever subsided, such excessive debility ensued, that the glimmering spark of life was with difficulty kept from extinction. It seemed for a period to be hovering between time and eternity. The pleasure I experience in being raised again, is indescribable. This renovated existence ought to be capable only of higher enjoyments. The delight of the family in my recovery gives new demonstration of their affection. But, my dear mother, great as are these claims, they are not the chief cause of my gratitude. He who hath seen fit to bring me from the borders of the grave, hath also shown the illusions of the world. Disen-

chanted, I view them in their real character and value. My life has been presented to me a dark scroll, on which there was not a single sentence of good, written, but was everywhere defaced with pride, vanity, indifference to religion, and ingratitude to Heaven. I saw myself standing on the verge of an awful eternity without a gleam of hope; in utter despair of salvation! Oh, my God! may I never forget the anguish of that moment. I had ever been a firm believer in Jesus Christ, but I felt an overwhelming consciousness that no personal application of His redeeming power had been made to me.

* * * * *

I am still in a state of probation; I can still call on His name, and in the hope that it will not be in vain. I am aware that resolves made on a sick bed frequently vanish like the morning cloud, before the renewed prospects and hopes of health. Oh! strengthen my resolutions, my dear mother, and pray that I may ever manifest the sincerity of my thankfulness.

Give my affectionate regards to my father. When my strength is restored, I will again write.

Your dutiful child,

C. L.

TO THE SAME.

LUDLOW STATION.

MY DEAR MOTHER:—

Let me review the providences, and pay the homage due to Infinite wisdom for the way in which I have been led. It pleased the Lord to visit me with his chastening rod. Again and again, I was prostrated with severe pain and weakness. My heart rebelled; I doubted His mercy and justice. The tempest was long and fearful. The billows rolled over me; and I was far from the view of a single earthly hope. But I was guided into the haven, and landed on the Rock of Ages!

Life now presents an entirely new aspect. No longer do my enjoyments depend on the incidents of a moment; my hopes now rest upon an unchangeable basis. My husband, my children, and my friends are dearer than ever to me; but the tie which binds them to me is purer and more rational. My dear father, mother, and sisters, let me implore you to pray earnestly that God may lead you in the way of all truth!

* * * * *

More than ever do I long to make you a visit. But I much fear Mr. Ludlow's business will again prevent it this autumn. Present my sincere love to Dr. King. His letters were a blessing to me. It was a fearful thought that God would leave me a victim to my own vanity and folly. In vain did friends try to comfort me. I could no longer disguise that my every action had been influenced by worldly motives, and had received its appropriate reward. What had I done for the glory of God, or for the salvation of a fellow mortal? I had depended on good works! Jesus had indeed been my helper, but not my Saviour! My miserable dependence for salvation was displayed with all its errors. Ōh, how had I imbibed the erroneous idea!

I have written on this subject to my beloved father, and I would write again and again; but should I offend him by my presumption, how at this distance could we ever be reconciled?

Adieu, my dear mother. With prayers for your happiness, I remain your affectionate daughter,

C. L.

TO GENERAL CHAMBERS.

My dear Father:—

Events continually occur which oblige us to procrastinate the long-contemplated visit to you. I wish to converse with you on the subject of religion, and time is rolling rapidly away. You, my dear father, taught me to love virtue and pray to God; and you considered me, and I esteemed myself, a Christian. I hope it is consistent with humility to believe myself a very different Christian now. How happy should I feel in being convinced that those endeared to me by the ties of blood had experienced a regenerated heart! I can never be sufficiently thankful for the gift of that grace which awakened me from a lethargy which was nigh unto death! Could I but live more to his glory!

* * * * *

That our heavenly Father may grant us all to drink of the waters of life freely, is the fervent supplication of your daughter.

C. L.

TO MRS. SCOTT.

LUDLOW STATION.

DEAR SISTER :—

Ever since my recovery, I have felt a serious determination, gently but earnestly, to warn my friends to attend to the " one thing needful." I am grieved at the thoughtlessness of all classes around us. Even this sacred day of rest is devoted to the pursuit of pleasure. Many attempt to excuse themselves from responsibility by supposing themselves too humble in position for their example to have any weight. How fatal a mistake! Every one, however unimportant his station, has some influence. There exists ample encouragement to pursue the path of religion, for in the consciousness of duty performed, we enjoy that secret satisfaction which, as the world gave not, neither can it take away. But after all we have done or can do, we are unprofitable servants. Salvation must be alone through Christ Jesus. Alas! the leaven of self-righteousness prevents thousands from relying simply upon Him. " We are better and safer than our neighbors." How flattering to our pride! Yet how vain to imagine that we can work out our own salvation, and not owe the glory to God. It is He who enables us to regulate the affections, and to say to the tumult of our passions, "Peace, be still!"

I have been awakened, as from a dream, and stand astonished at the depths of human weakness and unworthiness. Let us, as the disciples of Jesus, show compassion for the errors of our fellow-beings, yet be unalterably firm in the support and vindication of His blessed religion. What severe chastisement it required to bring me to God! How much pain and distress were necessary to humble me to the foot of the Cross! To His name be the glory!

* * * * *

You are thrown into society, where the tendency of things is to banish religion from your thoughts. Let me warn you against trifling away your precious hours. Let me entreat you to remember your immortal soul. As your elder sister, I solemnly and affectionately advise you.

* * * * *

C. L.

TO —— ——.

Ludlow Station.

Dear Mrs. E.:—

While the consciousness of your loss was fresh on your heart, the sympathy of friends would have served only to awaken sorrow in all its bitterness. It is useless to attempt to repress the indulgence of grief, when the truth is forced upon us, that loved ones are gone to the grave; and the heart must swell when memory recalls the countenance our eyes may never more dwell upon. But by this time, I hope you can reflect that the departure of our friend is but a prelude to our own, and that we will meet hereafter where care nor pain can ever reach us.

Could we look at events with that resignation Christians ought, and experience the assurance of meeting in another and better life that Christians ever do, it would not be in the power of any contingency to make us unhappy.

I have chosen this time, while your heart is softened by affliction, to intercede for your affectionate and sorrowing daughter. Our Saviour's parable of the prodigal son sets before us in a striking light, an example of the forgiveness and indulgence which a parent should exercise towards an erring child. That Being to whom we must all sue for pardon, has commanded us to forgive. How can we expect mercy if we exhibit to those who offend us, unrelenting displeasure.

Adieu. C. L.

TO —— ——.

Ludlow Station.

My Dear:—

The disciples of the Grecian moralists gloried in manifesting minute fidelity to the precepts and examples of their respective masters, and obeyed injunctions to the *letter* which were rigid and unpopular. We have reason to blush at the contrast which the lives of modern Christians exhibit. The light, instead of diffusing a steady and distinct splendor, scarcely glimmers in the socket; the salt scarcely imparts its savor, and the city on a hill, instead of being an object gloriously conspicuous, is obscured from view by the bramble of vanity and unbelief.

You inform me that you are happy to learn that I am still a Presbyterian. Why is the name of Presbyterian better than that of Methodist, which you seem to hold in so much contempt? If I am not a Christian, what will a name avail? I find no name given by man, to save me. May God grant that I may depend on no such stay for consolation! I hope I am deeply sensible of my weakness and imperfection. I desire to avoid all error of excess, or deficiency; but in conversation with any one, I am neither afraid nor ashamed to speak my sentiments. You know this is constitutional with me. I have not yet arrived at the confidence of an "exhorter," as you so gayly imagine. It would certainly give me pleasure to hear that you had advanced a little in that way, if it were to no higher dignity than "class-leader." Dr. S. informs me that you have become a great reader of theology. That you may add to your knowledge experience, and to your experience hope, is the prayer of

C. L.

Here we have to regret the loss of correspondence embracing a period of several years; especially that referring to the primitive condition of religion and society in the Northwestern Territory.

On a letter from Dr. King, a marginal note by Mrs. Ludlow says, "This is the forty-first letter in reply to mine." Unfortunately these were not applied for until too late to find them. They related to theological doctrine, and her own religious experience.

She deprecated the cold formalities of the Presbyterian

church; urged the necessity of greater liberty, zeal, and charity; lamented exclusiveness and sectarianism, and looked forward to the absorbing love of Jesus Christ as the only true and abiding bond of union.

TO MRS. CHAMBERS.

LUDLOW STATION.

MY DEAR MOTHER:—

* * How empty and unsatisfactory are the pursuits of the worldly! When I take my seat among those whose joys are those of travellers seeking a better country, from whose bosoms pride, ambition, and envy are banished; while magnanimity, love, and peace have filled their places, I feel as though the Millennium was begun! But there is an inconsistency with the religious I have always observed, and deeply deplore. I have seen the table of the Lord surrounded by his avowed followers; their whole demeanor expressive of fidelity and love, and declaring as it were, "Though all men forsake thee, yet will not I;" yet who, perhaps, a few days after, may be seen in the assemblies of vanity, at the card-table, and the theatre! Our blessed Lord said, "Strait is the gate and narrow is the way." Be not conformed to the world, but be ye transformed to the image of Christ. Though there are privileges our own consciences might allow, we should forego rather than cause a weak brother to offend, and consider it a duty to take the cross it might impose, and deny ourselves the indulgence. God requires the heart; but when it is offered at the shrine of every idol we chance to meet, it is useless to present the body to him. He had such perfect knowledge of us that he foresaw the evil of worldly indulgence to our spiritual welfare, and forcibly enjoined the necessity of self-denial.

* * * * *

Your affectionate

C. L.

TO MRS. DUNLOP.

LUDLOW STATION.

DEAR SISTER:—

Last evening, Mr. S. gave a farewell sermon at our house. It produced a powerful effect upon the audience. He exhorted them to seek diligently for the pearl of great price—that inestimable gem—that philosopher's stone, which can turn all things to gold.

* * * * * *

You say that Methodist, and Enthusiast, are terms applied to me. The idea of being subjected to ridicule as unfashionable, and enthusiastic, has no terrors for me. I am not only willing to endure this, but even "bonds and death," for the Lord Jesus! I blush to think what an unprofitable servant I am. Gladly would I introduce the subject of His sovereign grace in every company. To me, His name and His praise are the most precious of all themes. I pray, my dear Bella, that you may find the enlightening spirit of God! Then will you feel as having passed from darkness to light—then will your heart burn when speaking of your master, and experience deep interest in the salvation of blinded fellow mortals! As fidelity in friendship, constancy in love, modesty in woman, and filial affection, are worthy and respectable—so are ardor and zeal in religion!

C. L.

TO GENERAL CHAMBERS.

LUDLOW STATION.

MY DEAR FATHER:—

We are making preparations for an excursion into the forests of the Miami. Mr. Ludlow and myself, our two children and two nephews, with six men and a female servant, compose our party. Mr. Ludlow proposes to encamp one night, in order to give me some idea of the life of a *woodsman*. We have provided tents, blankets, provisions, and utensils for cooking. On our return, I will give you a description of our adventures.

Mr. Ludlow owns large tracts of lands on the Miami, and the Mad rivers. He describes the scenery as presenting beautiful extended plains, covered with the most luxuriant vines and strawberries; interspersed with clumps of trees; bounded by lofty forests, diversified by swelling hills, and through them flow the clearest streams. Frequently, to this picturesque display, are added flocks of deer, feeding at their ease undisturbed by the presence of man. Happy scenes of innocence and peace! Could you thus retain your features—could you remain unspoiled by the boasted changes of art—my husband and myself might participate in thy seclusion, and mingle our fawns with those of the wild deer!

Believe me, my father, no stream ever meandered through the plains of Miami, deeper or purer than my affection for you.

C. L.

TO THE SAME.

My dear Father:—

* * * * * * The Mad-river country has the reputation of being the garden-spot of Ohio. The river is neither broad nor deep, but flows with a rapid uniform current over a regular bed of white pebbles, and seldom exceeds its banks. It empties into the Great Miami at the town of Dayton, which Mr. Ludlow has lately laid out, and where he has mills, and other improvements.

The Miami also, is a beautiful river. It is not so broad as the Susquehanna, but measured by the scale of utility, it is a finer stream. Mr. Ludlow has land on it also, and has laid out the town of Hamilton near the fort. The river traverses a level, fertile country, and empties into the Ohio, twenty-one miles below Cincinnati. For nearly a mile after the junction, it seems emulous of prolonging its own course without mingling its waters with the majestic stream which scarcely deigns to notice its entrance—neither extending its banks, nor perceptibly deepening its channel in consequence.

This fine country, uniting in its interests and destinies with the Atlantic States, will one day extend its connections with the Pacific Ocean. By its central and retired position, it is sheltered from the tumults of war, unless, like unhappy Europe, it should be torn by intestine commotion. May that blessed period speedily arrive, "when nation shall no more rise against nation." Then the husbandman on the banks of the beautiful Ohio—with no outward ills to molest, or inward cares to annoy, will eat his fruit and drink his wine with unruffled joy and gladness.

* * * * * *

C. L.

TO MRS. CHAMBERS.

LUDLOW STATION.

MY DEAR MOTHER :—

I thank you sincerely for your many kind letters, for they are the only comforts I can receive from you at this distance. * * * I have the pleasure to inform you that my ague has taken its departure, we hope, forever. The last attack was early in June. I accompanied Mr. Ludlow to Hamilton on the day of its paroxysm. So air, exercise, and cheerfulness joined forces against it, and proved conqueror. Nine long months it has been my constant companion; but this time we put it to flight.

I thank you for the description of the "great meeting." You inform me you had no "disorder," no "crying out." My dear mother, I wish you could all have such zeal and deep feeling. How I would rejoice to hear that some of your dignified ladies, some of your stout-hearted Deists, or some of your good old formalists, had been heard crying out, "Men and brethren, what shall we do to be saved?" Our good Dr. King would then have mounted as on eagles' wings, and soared above the dull theology of the schools, and felt the transport of renovated youth on seeing the new-born sons and daughters of Zion.

* * * * *

C. L.

TO MRS. DUNLOP.

LUDLOW STATION, May 3d, 1802.

DEAR SISTER:—

* * It is now almost six years since I left you. Many changes and improvements have undoubtedly taken place. But when I do visit you, I would prefer meeting with all persons and things as I left them.

Dreams of the sweet morning of life, with what pleasure you return to my mind! In imagination I visit the house, the lawn, the locust and the willow; the garden where I passed so many happy hours; the little brook, rising in the mountain, rushing down the rock, and disappearing among the laurel; and the deep moan of the breeze as it sweeps through the lofty hemlock, that casts its funereal shade below.

* * * * *

Crossing the stream, I come in sight of the old cabin where Peggy lived. The whole is before me like a vivid dream. My father gay as ever; my mother caressing my own dear children; and you sitting under the great mulberry, conversing with Mr. Ludlow, while Mr. Dunlop, brother Benjamin, and myself are making the little folks of the group acquainted with each other. Dear sister, will this meeting ever be realized? But why should I cherish these alluring day-visions? Better to contemplate a higher and happier prospect, where we shall meet to part no more. Oh, may we all have that faith which triumphs over the temptations and vicissitudes of time, and enables us to bear the hope of meeting our best Friend, assured that where he is there may we be also!

* * * * *

C. L.

TO MRS. CHAMBERS.

Oct. 1st, 1803.

My dear Mother:—

The gloom occasioned by my husband's absence has been lightened by his frequent letters, and many anxious moments on his account relieved while perusing them. The religious change my feelings have undergone certainly conduces to enjoyments, even in a worldly sense. The society I am attached to now, tends to inspire peace, and breathe into my soul a composure for which I used to labor in vain. It is the result of resignation to the will of Heaven. The feelings and passions I once endeavored so unsuccessfully to suppress, are now brought into exercise, to co-operate in building up what they once destroyed. A consciousness that the will of God is displayed in every occurrence, must reconcile us to all events, however painful.

Should it please the Almighty to restore once more my husband to me and our children, I hope the blessing will make a suitable impression on us. I pray that our hearts may be softened with the lovely expression of gratitude which flowed from the lips of Jacob as he journeyed to Padan Aram, "If God will be with me, and will keep me in this way that I go, and will give me bread to eat, and raiment to put on, so that I come again to my father's house in peace, then shall the Lord be my God"—and how beautiful, in continuance, is the disposition to make a proper return!—"and of all that thou shalt give me, I will surely give the tenth unto thee!"

* * * * *

C. L.

CHAPTER V.

TO MRS. CHAMBERS.

LUDLOW STATION, Feb. 3, 1804.

MY DEAR MOTHER :—

How shall I begin my mournful communication? Your heart will sympathize but too tenderly and deeply in my afflictions, deprived as I am of the most amiable, affectionate, and indulgent of husbands. I am left alone and stricken to the earth! My children are too young to know their loss, and therefore excite the greater pity. My situation demands the exercise of all my reason and religion.

The Lord gave, and He hath taken away. May I be enabled to say, "Blessed be His name." I know the Judge of all the earth doeth right, whether we can comprehend it or not. This thought, I trust, will sustain me, whatever the bitterness of my portion. If I could experience a more perfect submission to the Divine will, I should feel more composed. But God sees our frail natures with compassion, and remembers that we are dust. As a father pitieth his children, so the Lord pitieth those who love him. The gracious promise that He will be a father to the fatherless and the widow's friend, is of all comforts at this time most precious. Oh, that I may be enabled to rest on Him for direction and hope!

In the many painful incidents which befell Abraham, David, and Job, I contemplate the unfailing support that sustained them. I discover that their sorrow was sanctified, and that they never forgot the mercies of God! Oh, that I could emulate their example, and *be still* beneath his chastening rod!

I know that my husband loved and feared the Lord. His heart was governed by the purest Christian principles ; and, without ostentation or display, his delight was in doing good. The poor will lament his loss, for he was their friend. Not yet recovered from the stunning blow, I find myself inquiring, is it real? Oh, my God, my merciful Father in Heaven, I thank Thee that I have the comforting hope of meeting him again at Thy right hand, no longer in sorrow and tears !

* * * * *

On Tuesday morning, Mr. Ludlow arose in his usual health, and on Saturday he left me for eternity. Oh, he is dead, my mother ! He is gone from me forever ! Language is inadequate to express the agony of such a moment !

* * * * *

I experienced every kind attention from my friends, Mrs. Gano, Mrs. Findlay, Mrs. Zeigler, Mrs. Stone, and Mrs. Allison. They were as sisters to me. Write to me, dear mother, words of consolation and advice. May the Lord be with me and my children !

Your afflicted daughter,

C. L.

Mr. Ludlow was not permitted to witness the wonderful results of the enterprise to which his untiring industry was directed in forwarding. That he had a prescience of its importance, is shown by his large entries of land—now noted for fertility and great value—in the region tributary to Cincinnati. The selection of town-sites when the territory was an unbroken forest, and where intimate knowledge of soil, timber, and natural outlet of country are necessary to eminent success, entitle him to no little credit for sound judgment and discriminating foresight.

Looking forward to a long life (but which was terminated ere the attainment of its prime), he felt that his immediate object was to lay the broad foundation of pecuniary fortune. Modesty was a well-known trait of his character. With an eye quick to discern, and energy to have applied, every measure conducing to the prosperity of the territory and the city, whose early progress was the adumbration of speedy greatness, he was himself indifferent to his own political advancement, and willing to wait at least, until the fulfilment of his present plans. Thus it is, without legislative record of the facts, his name is not known in a manner commensurate with his services to the infant colony and youthful state. His is not an anomalous case. The unwritten history of every community illustrates the point, that the most valuable men are not always, and indeed but seldom, in office.

Israel Ludlow was no politician in the clamorous sense of the term. He was a man for the times in which he lived, and possessed a peculiar fitness for the capacious sphere of his influence. The absence of such men in the necessitous condition of a struggling settlement explains the cause of premature decay and failure—their presence constitutes the main-spring of progress, the encouraging support of first puny effort, until accumulated strength affords the power of self-propulsion. He lived in a day when a citizen found in the extension of aid to the impoverished emigrant and his suffering family, ample scope for the exercise of the most generous heart-impulses. To him they could turn as a safe adviser and a substantial friend without fear of neglect. His life was illustrated by a series of practical benevolences, free from ostentation and the laudation of scarcely other than the recipients of his disinterested kindnesses.

It is related among the numerous anecdotes of him in the public journals of that time, that he one morning left home to be gone several days. Some while after bidding the family farewell, his voice was heard at the fence, calling to his wife, "Charlotte, do not forget the poor during my absence!" and turning his horse, he again proceeded on his way.

The shock created by the announcement of his death can be understood only in a new district, where the spareness of population and community of interest and friendship render conspicuous a valuable man, and his loss deep-seated and seemingly irreparable. The inhabitants joined the Masonic fraternity in paying the closing tribute of respect to his memory, and an oration was pronounced by the Hon. John Cleves Symmes.

The proprietors of Cincinnati reserved the square bounded by Main, Walnut, Fourth, and Fifth Streets for public use; the south half for a college and church; the north, for a court house and county offices. Near the church on Fourth Street, the body of Mr. Ludlow was deposited. A mercenary spirit, not satisfied with a perversion of trust, by which this space (filled with trees, and intended for a public square) was on its front lines covered with houses, in later years denied to the ashes of one of its donors, the further occupation of the small spot occupied by his hallowed monument. In the performance of the last sad rites of filial duty, his daughter, Mrs. McLean, had the remains placed under the foundation of the new church edifice, and a commemorative tablet fixed in the front wall.

Fifty Years Ago!

SONG OF THE WESTERN PIONEERS.[1]

A SONG of the early times out West, and our green old forest home,
Whose pleasant mem'ries freshly yet across the bosom come!
A song for the free and gladsome life in those early days we led,
With a teeming soil beneath our feet, and a smiling heav'n o'er head!
Oh, the waves of life danced merrily, and had a joyous flow,
In the days when we were Pioneers, Fifty years ago!

The hunt, the shot, the glorious chase, the captured elk or deer!
The camp, the big bright fire, and then the rich and wholesome cheer!
The sweet sound sleep at dead of night by our camp-fire, blazing high,
Unbroken by the wolf's long howl, and the panther springing by!
Oh, merrily pass'd the time, despite our wily Indian foe,
In the days when we were Pioneers, Fifty years ago!

We shunn'd not labor; when 'twas due, we wrought with right good-will;
And for the homes we won for them, our children bless us still.
We liv'd not hermit lives, but oft in social converse met;
And fires of love were kindled then that burn on warmly yet.
Oh, pleasantly the stream of life pursued its constant flow
In the days when we were Pioneers, Fifty years ago!

We felt that we were fellow-men; we felt we were a band
Sustain'd here in the wilderness by Heav'n's upholding hand.
And when the solemn Sabbath came, we gather'd in the wood,
And lifted up our hearts in pray'r to God, the only Good.
Our temples then were earth and sky; none others did we know
In the days when we were Pioneers, Fifty years ago!

[1] Composed by William D. Gallagher, Esq., and dedicated to the descendants of ISRAEL LUDLOW.

16

Our forest life was rough and rude, and dangers clos'd us round ;
But here, amid the green old trees, we freedom sought and found.
Oft through our dwellings wintry blasts would rush with shriek and moan,
We car'd not, tho' they were but frail; we felt they were our own!
Oh, free and manly lives we led, 'mid verdure or 'mid snow,
In the days when we were Pioneers, Fifty years ago!

But now our course of life is short; and as, from day to day,
We're walking on with halting step, and fainting by the way,
Another land, more bright than this, to our dim sight appears,
And on our way to it we'll soon again be Pioneers!
Yet while we linger, we may all a backward glance still throw
To the days when we were Pioneers, Fifty years ago!

CHAPTER VI.

TO M. A.

CINCINNATI, Sep. 9, 1805.

DEAR M. A.:—

Forget you, my friend; no, you will always be dear to my heart; but the state of my mind since the death of my husband, has rendered writing so great a task that I have given up all correspondence, except where business or duty made necessary its continuance.

I have endeavored to summon the fortitude of my nature. I know that sorrow cannot and ought not exempt me from the care my children demand; and I find that the exercise of my duties to them, arouses energies that might slumber in inaction. The little stranger, born four months after the death of his father, alleviates my grief by introducing a new object to divert my attention from melancholy retrospection. Often has the face of this unconscious babe been wet with tears, as I sat tracing the lineaments of his father in every feature. The merciful Disposer of all things has sustained me, and realized His presence to my soul.

* * * * *

I hope you have chosen the "better part." I know you are a believer, but as a venerable friend once said to me, are you a *follower* of Jesus? That you may become such, is the prayer of your friend.

C. L.

TO MRS. CHAMBERS.

CINCINNATI, September 10, 1805.

MY BELOVED MOTHER :—

I received my brother's letter containing the intelligence of our father's death. He too is gone. This stroke fell upon a heart still bleeding from recent loss. Dear, amiable father; my consolation is, that we shall meet again where sorrow and death are no more. This hope sustained me under a similar trial. I summoned my fortitude, but alas! how small my stock in proportion to the necessity of the case. In this dying world, God is our only help. I still looked forward to some period, when I should be enabled to visit the scenes of my youth, meet this beloved father again, show him the children God has given me, and receive his benediction. But I yet shall meet him. He is removed indeed, but the distance which separates us is diminished, not increased. Those frowning mountains do not now rise between us, and when we take our last journey, we shall mount the eternal hills on seraph's wings.

*　　*　　*　　*　　*

Your daughter,

C. L.

TO THE SAME.

July 5, 1806.

MY DEAR MOTHER :—

You have not answered my letter on the subject of coming west. I fear you do not sufficiently exert yourself to dissipate sorrow and low spirits. The indulgence of grief overclouds and destroys social enjoyment. It annihilates the charm of friendship, by throwing upon every object the gloomy clouds of our own minds; and not only renders ourselves, but every one interested for us, unhappy. It has pleased Heaven to enlighten me on this subject. I felt that an effort was necessary. I endeavored to mingle more with those whose conversation would have the power to withdraw my thoughts from myself and my troubles. It was in violence to my feelings, but I felt it a duty.

By the advice of friends I left a home—which, until the destroyer Death entered it, had been a paradise to me—and removed to Cincinnati. I strove to persuade myself that too much sensibility was weakness ; and as we are cast upon stormy elements, we should call religion and reason to our assistance. I began to reflect on my sources of consolation. My children are in the bloom of health, with perfect forms and good dispositions. The discipline and care of them is now the first object of my life. I can say with truth, my dear mother, " Hitherto the Lord hath helped me."

* * * * *

I have lately made a visit to Springfield. While there, I attended a "large Methodist meeting." I am aware that the prejudices of your education and habits of life would be excited, should I describe it to you. But I wish you had heard their fervent prayers, their stirring appeals, and eloquent rejoicings. They were greatly comforting to me.

* * * * *

C. L.

CINCINNATI, August 6, 1806.

JOURNAL.—In arranging papers, I find my long forgotten journal, written in days of bliss, never to return. The emotions occasioned by its perusal are indescribably painful. Ever lamented Ludlow! Time has, in a measure, allayed my anguish, but remembrance recalls his worth and impresses me with the magnitude of my loss.

Oh, indulgent Heavenly Father, I come as a child, confiding in Thy protecting care! I devote myself and my orphan children to Thee. Enable me to discharge my duty to them as a Christian parent. Enable me to rely firmly upon Thy promises in life, and in death grant us that hope in Thy son Jesus Christ which will elevate us superior to the pains of expiring nature.

* * * * *

SUNDAY MORNING.—Aug. 15. * * Why should I continue this journal? few striking incidents transpire. But my children may be interested in turning over these leaves, when the hand which traced them is cold in death. Ungrateful being that I am, why should I repine? Blessed with health, and a hope which this world can neither give nor take away. * * * * * * May I live to His glory who has so bountifully enriched me! Much cause have we to blush for our wandering hearts!

"Prone to wander, Lord, I feel it;
Prone to leave the God I love."

Heavenly Father, seal my heart with Thy Holy Spirit! May I persevere in Thy service, and rest with unshaken hope on Thy promises! I will never leave Thee nor forsake Thee!

September 28.—On my return from prayer meeting this morning, I found the family assembled for breakfast. Kneeling with them I solicited the gifts of grace, wisdom, and the Lord's protecting care.

At church to-day my seat commanded a view of the prison. Deplorable state of man, that renders such a place necessary. Unfortunate beings, thus to be deprived of liberty. Oh, most unhappy fact, that their minds, through ignorance and vice, are incapable of virtuous exertion. Benighted and grovelling, they sink to a level with the brute. My heart was touched with deep compassion, and my prayers were offered for them. * * * * *

To-day Mr. Wallace preached from these words, "Choose you this day whom you will serve; whether the God which your fathers served, which were on the other side of the flood, or the gods of the Amorites in the land which ye dwell; but as for me and my house, we will serve the Lord." He was eloquent and interesting, but there were few to hear him.

* * * * *

My mother closed her book, inquiring, "Charlotte, what are you writing?" "A few casual thoughts, mamma, just as they occur, for my own amusement." "Had you not better notice the recent commotions of the town?" "If you desire it," replied I. * * *

A report has been circulating, that Aaron Burr, in conjunction with others, is forming schemes inimical to the peace of his country; and that an armament and fleet of boats are now in motion on the Ohio; and that orders have actually arrived from head-quarters for our military to intercept and prevent its progress down the river. In consequence of these orders, cannon are planted on the bank, and a sentinel stationed on the watch. The light-horse commanded by Capt. Furguson, have gallantly offered their services; and Capt. Carpenter's company of infantry are on the alert. Cincinnati has quite the appearance of a garrisoned town. A tremendous cannonading was heard yesterday, and we all thought Burr and his armament had arrived; but it was only a salute to a fleet of *flat boats*, containing military stores for the different stations on the river.

* * * * *

First day of the new year, 1807. Another year has commenced its round. May we improve our time! May we spend this year as though it were our last! We live too much in the eyes of the world, too little to our own conscience, and too little to our own satisfaction. We are more anxious to appear happy than to be really so.

How true those remarks of Knox! How inestimable that independence which can nobly study self-approbation, without the sacrifice daily offered by weak understandings to the opinion of the world.

* * * * *

SABBATH.—Retiring to my room this morning to read the Bible, I opened the book at the history of Saul, and read the address of Samuel to him. We may suppose Saul young, athletic, and graceful in person, with dignified deportment, and intelligent mind. His father, though not numbered with the rulers, was a "mighty man of power." I suppose wealthy in his circumstances, and influential in his counsels. To his father, Saul was united both as a son and a friend; perhaps he was an only child.

The amiability of his answer to Samuel's first address, impresses us with a favorable opinion of his modesty and ingenuousness. When Samuel said, "And on whom is all the desire of Israel? is it not on thee?"

Saul answered, "Am not I a Benjamite, the smallest of the tribes of Israel, and my family the least of all the families of the tribe Benjamin? Wherefore, then, speakest thou so to me?" Benjamin, that brave but almost exhausted tribe, and his family the least, the fewest in number, where was his mighty influence that all Israel should look to him? Saul resigned all to the great Disposer of events, and returned to his father filled with the spirit of God.

It is mysterious that one so highly favored should disappoint all our hopes, and degrade the station he seemed formed to adorn. But so it was, and the train of painful consequences composing his history, is an impressive warning to all in power. His first and last great error was departure from God. Samuel in his pathetic oration to the people assures them, "If ye will fear the Lord, and serve Him, and obey His voice, and not rebel against the commandment of the Lord, then shall both ye and also the king who reigneth over you continue following the Lord your God."

What a solemn lesson is here! May it animate me to more serious prayer! I am not a prophet to whom a nation looks up; but I am a *mother!* and God forbid that I should sin against Him in ceasing to pray for my children!

Feb. * * During a long continuation of cold weather, clouded atmosphere, and cheerless prospects, how pleasing the recollection of a serene sky, a full moon, and the sparkling brilliancy of an evening in May! On such a night, David contemplated the glory of the heavens when he exclaimed, What is man that Thou art mindful of him?

This song of the sweet singer of Israel is supposed to have been composed immediately after the overthrow of Goliah and the army of the Philistines. David, the hero of the exploit, in the voluptuous court of Saul, would be compelled to join in the revelling consequent on the victory. But awake only to the admiration of nature and nature's God, he would fly the first moment of relaxation from things with which his heart had so little affinity. Perhaps in a grove near the foot of Mount Olivet, he found a shelter from the busy throng; and there, with the harp as his only companion, by the moon's splendor, and amid the glories of an Eastern sky, he poured forth in devotional rhapsody the overflowings of his soul to Him who was the source of his power and the Rock of his confidence. Contrasting this scene with the one just quitted, no wonder he exclaimed, What is man that Thou art mindful of him, or the son of man that Thou visiteth him ?

April 7. * * General and Mrs. Mansfield expressed surprise that I was not a more frequent visitor at Ludlow Station. Dear, favorite place! Shall I ever again become its occupant? Ah! not its trees and shrubs, its hills and limpid springs, its orchards, flowery banks, and picturesque ravines alone endeared it to me. My tears flow not for these. I mourn the loss of one whose presence gave each object its enchantment. That charm is gone; the others are now to me wild, solitary, and unmeaning!

Oh, thou God of life, of love, order, and beauty, lead my brighter hopes to the anticipation of that place where all is permanent, where no vicissitudes can come, no pain disturb!

* * * * *

Our desolate church is yet without a pastor, and our elders and members grow each day more cold and lifeless. A stranger preached this morning. He urged the necessity of unity among Christians, lamented the opposition and want of brotherly love as obstacles to the progress of true piety, and proved in a beautiful manner this to be the "dust," spoken of in prophecy, Zion was to shake from her garments.

* * * * *

April 14.—The weather continues mild. I have had men employed in the garden. It was ever a favorite amusement with me. This season neglected cannot be repaired throughout the year. It is April with my children; let me plant in their young minds the seeds of virtue and religion, and with maternal care prevent the growth of noxious principles.

June 3.—I have passed the day with my excellent friends, Mrs. Dr. Allison and Mrs. General Taylor, of Newport, Ky. It was a day of rational enjoyment. In the common intercourse of friends, too much valuable time is lost in trifling topics, which might be devoted to better purpose.

* * * * *

Mr. K. on Saturday discoursed from the text, "Prepare to meet thy God." Oh, heavenly Father, reveal thyself to us in love! Withhold not for one moment Thy comforting power. Without Thee, no possession would be valuable, no pursuit profitable, no day happy. I look beyond this world rapturously to the joys of eternity with Thee!"

*   *   *   *   *

SABBATH.—July 10.—How destructive to the real enjoyment of this day is the ceaseless visiting, so much practised by those destitute of resources within themselves; resorting to any expedient to while their happy riddance from themselves; destroying thought wherever they go! How persons of even ordinary taste and refinement can squander the Lord's day in a dull routine of riding and visiting, is to me inexplicable!

*   *   *   *   *

The conflict is over, and our pastor, Mr. Davis, has departed for a better world. Never was more perfect resignation, more exemplary piety exhibited. Not a murmur, or scarcely a moan escaped his lips, though his sufferings were acute. His countenance beamed with the animation and hope usual when addressing his audience from the pulpit. His tone of voice, his manner the same; polite, gentle, and serene to the last moment.

His kneeling wife, with his hands pressed to her heart, supplicated Heaven for resignation. Behold in me the reality of all I have told you. I go the way of all the living. Soon will the way be yours; and prepare to meet thy God. Rev. James Kemper preached the funeral sermon. It was a discourse well suited to the occasion.

TO MRS. CHAMBERS.

CINCINNATI, Aug. 7, 1807.

MY DEAR MOTHER:—

When my children are assembled around me, looking to me alone to guide, advise, and provide for them, the loss of their father, with a sense of my own incompetency to supply his place, excites the deepest degree of pity for them. How interesting the study of their different dispositions and tastes! One has energy united with gentleness of manner; another is volatile, yet assiduous; another combines imagination with judgment; another, bearing the peculiar impress of the country, is inclined to be turbulent and daring. May I live to see them pursuing the ways of virtue, and growing in the fear and love of the Lord! I took them out yesterday to our once happy home. Col. Jared Mansfield, who at present occupies it, is a gentleman of extensive scientific knowledge and charming urbanity. Mrs. Mansfield is highly intelligent and interesting, and possesses the most noble qualities of head and heart, in beautiful harmony with the feminine and domestic virtues. In their society, I passed one of those days my soul loves.

* * * * *

I have written to sister Bella. I hope she has become reconciled to the death of her little daughter. Why should we wish one dear to us—who has passed the dark barrier of death, and entered into the light and joy of eternity—back again? I pray that she may acquiesce in the will of Him who gave, and who has the right to take away.

C. L.

TO BENJAMIN CHAMBERS.

Sept. 1, 1808.

DEAR BROTHER:—

That without revelation, man would have been capable of discovering one omnipotent, omnipresent, and eternal God, I cannot believe; or that creation would have occurred to his mind, seems improbable. I think the idea of matter being eternal, would have been the most natural suggestion. And man would have surely felt himself inferior to animals of greater strength and agility, had not a supernatural impression of his mental superiority been made on the animal creation. But that power who called all things into being, predetermined that man should know Him by whom he was formed, and when created should have such manifestations of his Creator, that the idea could never be lost, but should be supported by tradition when written records were unattainable.

We sink into sheer hypothesis in supposing a family or nation without the idea of a God. But in some countries, for want of written record, it has degenerated into polytheism and fable. A modern deist—

I mean one who denies the truth and necessity of revelation—is more inexcusable than the heathen. It is said, they glorified him not as God, but became vain in their imaginations, boasting in human reason and perplexing subtleties, until, enveloped in darkness, they became impenetrable to the simplicity of truth.

The surrounding nations must have learned much from the Hebrews, though they continued to practise the abominable rites of idolatry. Some individuals among them, held in high esteem, lost popularity, and finally life, by attempting reformation. Devoted to war and rapine, mankind was daily inventing new fables, new mischiefs and wickedness, until the advent of Jesus Christ introduced a glorious era. No wonder that heaven and earth united in hallelujahs! Then, and not until then was light, and peace, and love shed abroad. "Go into all the earth," was a command incomprehensible even to whom it was given. "The Gentiles shall come to Thy light, and kings to the brightness of Thy rising." Zion is now extending her dominion, and the nations shall be blessed. But, my dear brother, this is not done by studying the stars! Comets, suns, and planets are grand objects to a Christian philosopher, who can see with the eye of faith.

* * * * *

I can scarcely refrain from pronouncing that person destitute of common sense, who doubts the truth and necessity of revelation. He might as well deny the laws of matter, proved by a thousand demonstrations, and witnessed in everything around us.

* * * * *

Adieu, my dear brother. Let us, who believe, rejoice in the truth as contained in the Bible.

C. L.

CHAPTER VII.

Mrs. Ludlow mourned her husband during six years of widowhood. After much serious consideration of the subject, and with the advice of friends, she gave her hand in marriage to the Reverend David Riske. In this important step, she was influenced chiefly by the desire to secure a religious guardianship for her children and a wider sphere of usefulness for herself.

Mr. Riske was an Irish gentlemen, educated at the University at Edinburgh, of good personal appearance, and courteous accomplishments. He was a minister of the Associate Reformed Presbyterian Church, and had in his charge, at one and the same time, three congregations in as many several townships.

Shortly after this marriage, Mrs. Riske made Ludlow Station again her residence. Here were born her two daughters Ruhamah and Charlotte. In the seclusion of country life, as the wife of a clergyman, she visited her neighbors in affliction, and continually exercised that charity which Christian humility and a woman's heart suggested, and bountiful harvests enabled her to consummate.

TO MRS. DUNLOP.

LUDLOW STATION, June 7, 1810.

MY DEAR SISTER :—

Two extremes, equally fatal to our peace, we are admonished to avoid: despising the chastisements of God, or fainting under them. Those who have been objects of social endearment mourn the loss of friends with a degree of poignancy too often precluding consolation. I trust it is not so with you, but that you are enabled to arouse from inaction by acknowledging the sovereignty of God. What He doeth we know not now, but shall know hereafter. Soon the short period of this life will be succeeded by an eternity in mansions of bliss.

* * * * *

Walking to visit a neighbor last week, I saw old Mrs. H. before me. I quickened my pace to overtake her. After the usual salutation, I expressed a hope that she was now more comfortable in her circumstances. "Oh!" said she, "I was just thinking as I walked along, of the goodness of God. Mysterious are His providences! While we struggle against them, the conflict is severe indeed. He has taught me submission. I am not only resigned, but contented and happy." I expressed pleasure in seeing her so cheerful. "I find," she continued, "much depends on the way we take trouble. When I was young, I thought everything must prosper; and with diligence there was no danger but that we should be rich. But alas! a long train of misfortunes which our industry could not remedy, overtook us, made us fretful, miserable, and ungrateful. The few comforts we had reserved, were embittered by disappointments. One thing after another went; at length our dear babe sickened and died. We were then on our journey to 'French Broads.' Before her death, we sought admittance at some of the solitary cabins on the road. But hearts familiar with wretchedness, become hardened. No one suffered us to enter, no one offered a sympathizing look. The child had not the solace of one day's rest; our circumstances not allowing us to lay by. She died in my arms, under a tree on the bank of a creek. There, a kind wagoner and my husband and I, buried her; and laying some broken wood over the little grave, we were constrained to take a last farewell. She was one of the loveliest creatures

I ever saw; and though but two years of age, seemed conscious of our distress, and suppressed her complaints, fearing to augment my sorrow. We proceeded on our journey, and after a tedious time with bad roads, deep waters, and scanty fare, reached our intended home. Misfortune pursued us there, and becoming dissatisfied, we set out for Cincinnati. Our children since that period, have been born in poverty. They are healthy and industrious, and have an open world before them. My poor husband never ceased to lament his change of circumstances, and new schemes awakened new hopes that were never realized. Although he was capable and temperate, he never acquired resignation. After his death, I came to the country in search of *rest.* My cabin is comfortable, and by the help of our wheel, chickens and pigs, we are enabled to live. We now have time to read the Bible, to go to meeting, and see our friends, and are under no apprehension of arrest. The pride which induced us to sigh for riches, is gone, and we acknowledge that the Lord has directed all in mercy. Ah! He knows me better than I know myself."

This interesting narrative brought us to our place of separation, where I gave my hand to the good woman. The family I was going to console for the loss of a husband and father, I found cheerfully disposed; which proved the truth of dear Mrs. H.'s observation, "Much depends on the way we take trouble." She and her children were only separated from a tyrant, and had more sense than to affect sorrow they did not feel. After a short visit, I called on another poor neighbor, who also was in trouble. Here indeed was an opportunity of seeing how adequate is the power of grace in reconciling us to affliction. A boy thirteen years of age was supported in a chair by pillows and blankets. His mother with his head on her bosom, kindly soothed him. Piteous moans evinced his suffering. He was frightfully reduced by pain and long confinement; and his mind was even more imbecile than his body. He had generally four or five convulsions in the course of the day; and in this situation he had been for five years.

The mother spoke of the Lord's goodness in enabling them to bear their trials without murmuring, and observed that it might have been worse. "How many are in raving madness; but thank the Lord," said she, "the light of His countenance has supported us, and He knows what is best for us."

Here, my dear Bella, is a lesson of wisdom for us all. What is a tranquil exit of nature in comparison with this? You have lost a beloved daughter. Resign her to him who gave. Rather be thankful that she was taken from evils to come.

Your sister,

C. Ludlow Riske.

Journal.—Sabbath morning. On again opening this, I was impressed with the reflection that Time advancing, is unsullied. Like these fair pages, no trace of human weakness or imperfection has yet impressed either. Oh Thou in whose hand is every event of my future, enable me to pass from day to day pure and unoffending, and impart wisdom and light to guide me on the way!

* * * * *

My much valued friend, Dr. King, has gone to his rest. I mourn his loss. The endearing appellation of daughter from himself and Mrs. King, had an influence on my early affections, and I recall with pleasure the happy hours passed with them in the days of youthful fancy, when all I saw was pleasing to my heart. My father is also gone. I love and revere his memory, and delight in thinking of the times when he directed his children to useful studies, and early taught them to suppress every appearance of severity of remark. He led his children to adore the wisdom in the universal harmony of nature, and to patiently submit to the dispensations of Providence. Having been in military life for some time, a martial enthusiasm was the language of his soul. God was his general, his shield, and his fortress. With our mother, we reflected on objects beyond the limit of this world in the wonders of Grace. Thus, without preconcerted plan, they brought us up in the nurture and admonition of the Lord. * *

By what an infinite variety of benefits is religion recommended! It gives a charm to solitude, a bond to charity, forms a barrier to the wanderings of the imagination, controls the passions, and directs the reason!

Bible and missionary societies are exciting much interest. We know that the Lord is all powerful. We also know that He makes use of temporal means to accomplish His designs. These societies may be the means of spreading the light of the gospel more rapidly. Even amongst ourselves, many are destitute of the Scriptures, and have but one Bible for each house.

I remember when about sixteen years of age, feeling an unusual depression of mind. It was on the Sabbath, and I was in my room alone. Nearly at sunset, after having passed the day in reading, I was overcome with a horror of impending misfortune. Kneeling by the side of my bed, with the Bible open before me, I prayed that whatever calamity should befall me, it might not be estrangement from God. I bless and adore His holy name. My prayer has been heard in every trial, and I have been led to trust implicitly on His promises, and to build upon the Rock which nothing can move.

May 2, 1815.—This morning was mild, and all was bright. Delightful season! Its succession to dreary winter adds much to its real beauty. I arose early, and participated in the general pleasure. I was filled with thankfulness and tranquillity, and impressed with the presence of superintending Divine intelligence. How pleasing to dwell in the indulgence of habitual adoration! How grand to contemplate omnipotent power from the minutest plant to the distant star! Mind, like the body, requires aliment, and the resources of nutrition are as various for one as the other.

May 10.—Having had for a length of time, an ardent desire to establish a Bible society in our neighborhood, I requested the attendance of a few Christian friends on an appointed day, and sent a messenger for some miles around to invite all who felt disposed, to unite with us in effecting this object. The subject, I suppose, exciting little interest, no one came.

I went to the room appropriated to the purpose at the designated hour, and seated myself at the table. I was filled with the august presence of the Invisible One whose eye searcheth all hearts. After reading a portion of Scripture from the Prophet Joel, beginning at the verse, "Fear not, O land! Be glad and rejoice, for the Lord will do great things," I closed the book, and prayed for Divine aid and blessing. Opening a blank book, I made a minute of the meeting, where only the Lord and myself were present.

I sent word to the neighbors that the Bible Society would meet again that day two weeks. When the time arrived, thirty women were present, and the society was organized.

* * * * *

These associations appear to me sent by the Almighty to prepare the world for some great event. Prophecy alludes to providences which are to effect great changes in the latter days. And our Lord speaks of distressing persecutions, in consequence of which, He informed his disciples, "The love of many would wax cold."

* * Many will probably be compelled to declare their attachment to the Redeemer's cause at the hazard of their lives, or to join His enemies. How can we better assist the rising generation and those yet unborn, than by placing the Bible in the hands of every one? The time may come when none will be printed, and those that remain, will be more precious than the gold of Ophir! when there will be a dearth, not of corn or of wine, but of the word of God. May we improve this time of plenty, and have abundance, should famine ensue!

O God, increase and diffuse Thy word, and accompany it with efficacious demonstration, throughout the globe, and grant that all persons may contribute willingly to the advancement of Thy kingdom by giving that money to good purposes which is now squandered in vanity, thoughtlessness, and crime!

Twelve o'clock. Night.—I cannot forbear employing a few moments to record my great obligation for the delightful serenity of soul and the clear manifestation of God's pardoning love I have this day enjoyed. Heavenly Father, accept my gratitude for all Thy favors! I thank Thee for Thy blessings to my family, and our friends, and to the nation. I adore and praise Thee, O God of peace!

Sabbath.—I endeavor to make this a day of intellectual enjoyment to the household; a day of rest and religious instruction. I have found the address of Christ to the disciples on the Mount, an excellent portion of scripture for an evening exercise. Collecting the younger part of the family, I sometimes read it with them, each one a paragraph, without interruption, until the sentiment is finished; and thus until the whole is read. I then inquire what characters the Lord pronounced blessed; what is said respecting good works; what concerning anger; what in reference to the commandments; what of swearing; concerning our enemies; alms; prayer; forgiveness of injuries; laying up treasures, &c.: in this way, going through this perfect system of morality. As an epitome of the Christian religion, this sermon should be early fixed in the minds of children.

Nov. 7. * * Our neighbor, Mr. M., who has been sick for several weeks, sent for us an hour before the dawn of day. We found him engaged in prayer. The thought of his wife, his children, and his own soul, alternately agitated him. After inquiry, instruction, and prayer, Mr. Riske baptized him, and the sacred ordinance of the Lord's Supper was administered to himself and wife. His previous restlessness and perplexity entirely ceased; and with firm confidence in a blissful immortality, he resigned his soul to his Maker.

* * * * *

TO ——— ———

LUDLOW STATION, 1815.

MY DEAR DAUGHTER:—

* * I know from experience the dangers of the period through which you are passing. * * In a few years you will occupy the point where I am now, and those in succession, will press upon your footsteps. He who gave us this frail tenement has withheld from us the knowledge of the time of its dissolution. This should be a motive to vigilance and sobriety, and as to-morrow is a period upon which none of us have any claim, it is important that we should fill up the measure of duty assigned to us, to-day. Honor the early instructions and

example of your friends, and strive to convey just estimates of your understanding, by a conduct as blameless, and as near perfection as possiblė. Seek light, my dear child, from Him who only can guide you in the way of all truth. You are far distant from your only earthly parent; but your Heavenly Father is equally near in all places. My trust is that He will never forsake you. May He return you in safety to us!

* * * * *

Your mother,
C. L. R.

TO MRS. DUNLOP.

June 2, 1816.

DEAR BELLA:—

To our dear sister R., the death of her son has been a severe trial. Her loss excites the deepest sympathy of her friends here. I pray that she may be enabled to look beyond the horizon of present afflictions to clearer skies; and that the power of religion will soften her grief, and bring peace to her bosom. But at present she is inconsolable.

* * * * *

I am rejoiced to hear that Sabbath school instruction is gaining interest in your neighborhood. I hope those who are anxious for the success of the cause will unite their strength. Infant schools should certainly claim the attention of parents and teachers. Children demand amusement and employment as soon as they are able to distinguish objects; and this propensity is retained through life.

* * * * *

What object on earth so precious as our children? Their souls are as dear to us as our own; and to train them in the fear and the love of God is a duty equally binding and delightful. More perfectly to fulfil this, Sabbath schools should be encouraged. May the Lord give you zeal in every such undertaking!

C. L. R.

TO THE SAME.

June 19, 1816.

Dear Bella:—

* * Upon the subject of giving tokens to the partakers of the Lord's Supper, I once thought as you do; but consideration of the subject, reconciled me to the form. Religion is not the effect of excited passions, but of convinced reason, and there is no need of haste in this important affair. On joining the church, I was pleased that my views of sacred things were to be exhibited to those who were accounted judges, and that I was going forward to the Lord's table, not only from my own hope of interest in Christ Jesus, but after a candid examination of my faith by others. The token was then one of fellowship. The Lord says that we must come in at the door, make the good confession before witnesses, and not climb over the wall.

Once in our church, after tokens had been distributed, and the second table filling, a young man arose, and spoke aloud, "This is not a Presbyterian table—it is the Lord's table, and as one of His disciples I shall go forward and partake;" and he took a seat. Mr. Wilson, after a short silence, said to him in a low but emphatic voice, "We have done what we consider to be our duty; we leave the rest to God and your own soul." He then proceeded as though nothing had occurred.

Let us respect the regulations which the wisdom and prudence of those who have the rule over us consider right to maintain. But this standard of law should be as near Divine authority as possible. I feel thankful that you have desired to "Do this in remembrance of Him." Quench not the Spirit; and that God may bless you with increasing desire, until you have grown to the true stature in Christ Jesus, is the prayer of your affectionate

C. L. R.

Journal.—May, 1816. * * O Heavenly Father, infinite is Thy power! How inexhaustible Thy goodness! How boundless Thy love! I praise and adore Thee, Thou sustainer of hope and confidence! When difficulties occur, Thy hand removes them. When painful circumstances arise, it is Thee, O wonderful Counsellor! who gives us resignation and tranquillity. I thank and praise Thee that Thou hast said Pray without ceasing, that importunity will not offend Thee.

* * The shades of the night, the dawning of the morning, from Thee have their origin, and their continuation. The return of the seasons, the splendor of the firmament, the fruitfulness of the earth, the mind of man, all show Thy creative and sustaining power, and that Thou art the being Thy word reveals, the only living God, the great Jehovah!

Comfort, Oh, comfort Thy people! Build up the broken walls of Jerusalem; restore Zion, "Make its walls salvation and its gates praise." Fill the earth with the glad tidings until all will rejoice in Thee.

Sept. 28, 1816.—With joy I record the goodness of the Lord. At length a female association is formed in Cincinnati, as an auxiliary to the American Bible Society, lately instituted in New York. * *

Oh, may the Lord instruct us in wisdom, and bring us under His control, and may all our exertions be directed to His glory!

I was gratified in meeting many friends willing to engage in the great and interesting object of diffusing the blessings of the Word. Assist us in telling of a risen Saviour, and increase our zeal in Thy service! In Thy strength, O Lord, we act, resting firmly on Thy promise that where two or three unite in asking, Thou wilt give! We pray Thee to preside in all our councils. Let not our unworthiness cause Thee to withhold the light of Thy countenance. * * * * *

The Female Bible Society met to-day at the house of Mrs. B. Mason. In compliance with her invitation, we shall continue to hold our monthly meetings there. He who has said, A cup of cold water offered in my name shall not lose its reward, will remember this offering of love, this dedication of her house to His service.

* * * * *

This morning, the Rev. Mr. Thomas met with us at six o'clock in Judge Burke's church. I had informed him of my wish to assemble the young men of our immediate neighborhood every Sabbath morning for the purpose of reading the Scriptures, and forming in them a desire for intellectual culture. * * It was a time of great seriousness.

O Lord, to Thee we raise our hearts in hope of a blessing on these meetings! * * * * *

Desiring to forward the operations of the new missionary society, Mrs. Judge Burnet, Mrs. Kinney, and myself took upon ourselves the labor esteemed disagreeable—that of soliciting funds for its treasury. Several incidents occurred, helping to assure us that the Lord had made the way plain! Many cheerfully contributed. One young gentleman read the preamble to the constitution, and subscribed ten dollars. On receiving the money, I looked at the signature, and found it to be that of James Glenn.

On being ushered into the drawing-room of a friend, where our expectations had been very sanguine, we found a coterie of those who are viewed as *first* among the various circles of our city. We were received with great courtesy. There were two generals, one judge, one colonel, and the lady of the house. After the usual common-place remarks, we mentioned the business of our visit. But, alas, all was wrong! The measure was deprecated; the idea was absurd; the times were too hard. But harder were their hearts! Even the lady refused! In vain did Mrs. Kinney, Mrs. Burnet, and myself portray the necessity of sending the gospel to the destitute. We spoke of the shortness of life, the blessings of serving the Lord with our wealth, and the earnest call for uniting our efforts in the good work! But the opposition becoming too loud for us to be heard, we left, mutually astonished at each other, I suppose; they, that we should take the trouble to become solicitors for a cause so far beneath them—and we, at their slowness of heart to believe!

A few evenings after, we were invited to an elegant party at this same house! The superabundance there expended, would have shed lustre on the name of this hospitable citizen had it been in the form of a donation to the missionary society. Ah, how many invincible barriers present where generosity is required to aid this cause—for which men have sacrificed life and all that was dear to them—the cause for which our glorious Redeemer relinquished the splendor of Heaven, and became poor, not having where to lay His head—that blessed, peace-speaking religion, which has given us all our most valued enjoyments, rendering existence delightful, and death without terror!

Yesterday the heat of the sun was great, and the vegetation suffered for want of moisture. About the middle of the afternoon, the wind arose; the dust ascended in columns and enveloped the town, exhibiting a faint simile to the Simoom. The sound of distant thunder was a sound of gladness. A dark cloud appeared in the northwest horizon, and in a few moments, large drops of rain sprinkled the pillars of dust. The thunder increased, a hard shower cleared the atmosphere, the dust was consolidated, and things animate and inanimate were refreshed.

How good is the Lord! While foreboding man imagined all the bad consequences of drouth, unwholesome vapors, languor, sickness, accidental fires, exhausted cisterns, and general ruin, lo, instead of the heavens being "brass over our heads, and the earth iron under our feet" for our sins, the Lord showered down blessings in the former, and in the latter, rain!

Oh, Thou advocate with the Father, one shower is yet wanting—a shower of Divine grace; an outpouring of Thy spirit upon this city! Condemn us not like the barren fig-tree, while we languish and become unfruitful. The cares of this world involve us in a cloud of ingratitude and unprofitableness. The showers of grace and of nature are equally under Thy control. Thou art the Rock whence issue the rivers of life!

* * * * *

August. * * I was awakened last night by the sound of distant music. The effect was enchanting. As it approached, images long since sunk in oblivion were restored, and produced harmonious and sublime associations.

I arose to listen whence came the melody, and found that to Echo, tossed in rich undulations around the hills, I was indebted for the symphony. The mail-carrier, privileged to announce his coming with the bugle, was enjoying the fine effect of its clear note. The night was far advanced; the moon was near the zenith, and profound was the silence in all quarters of the town.

Mutual is the confidence felt by the citizens in the protecting arm of Providence and in each other. Such is the general health, peace, and prosperity originating in the goodness of God among us, that the language of my heart was, "Behold a miracle is here."

The contentious and the peaceful, the indolent and the active, the infidel and the believer, share alike the blessings of repose and protection under the administration of that beneficent Being who causeth the sun and the rain to descend upon the evil and the good. The silver trumpet of the gospel is awakening the moral world to universal jubilee. Under its sweet reverberations, the whole earth shall be one splendid city, illuminated by the presence of Christ, our king! And the last trump, sonorous and shrill, will awake the dead and call the nations forth to judgment!

Jan. 12, 1817. Sabbath morning.—The day is dawning. The traveller benighted in a wilderness, in peril from wild beasts, in peril by land and by water, almost despairing, and overcome by fatigue, views with delight the dawning day. Fresh resolutions invigorate him, and difficulties lessen. Equally precious is one ray of light to the benighted soul. * * * * * *

O God! dispel the darkness of despair. Dawn upon the unregenerate heart, and as the light of this day increases, so may Thy grace increase in my soul. Enable me to rejoice without ceasing. Though clouds darken my horizon, if Thou art present, I am sustained. Without Thee, every step increases the uncertainty. But I have found Thee near and compassionate. It is to Thee, O glorious Redeemer! we owe all that is worthy in life, and sustaining in death. Thy hand can direct us safely; and nothing will annoy, nothing confound, us. We are clothed, warmed, and fed by Thee, and finally in Thy mansions of rest we shall be received to a blissful eternity.

To Thee I resign my children. Choose their changes, and make the path of duty plain before them. Spare them from the rude storms of life. Impress upon them the importance of truth, and vouchsafe to them the everlasting inheritance that fadeth not away. May we all meet in Thy kingdom! The avaricious seek gold; the ambitious, applause; the voluptuary, pleasure; but be Thou their portion forever. * *

A May Day Address to my Horse, aged twenty-three years.

Hail! gentle Prince, this blessed first of May
With pastures green, sweet, succulent and gay,
Thy kind saluting "Ho, Ho," meets my ear
As welcome in thy sight I still appear.
Now all the blasts of stormy winter's flown,
Trot round these fields, and call them all your own,
Crop the rich clover, drink the meadow streams,
Bask in the sun, or shelter from its beams;
These banks and streams, this grass and shade are yours,
Long as your life and form a horse endures.
When young, with grand contour and gallant mien,
You whirled the chaise or trod the martial plain,
Undeviating, ardent, firm and true,
No confidence abortive placed in you.
The smallest impulse of the slackened rein
Would speed the journey, or the course restrain;
No rash alloy your generous courage knew,
On life's fair path ne'er once regardless flew.
Goodness or virtue in a man or horse,
The same its effect, as the same its source.
So fair your fame, so high your honor stood,
Posterity will call you Prince the Good!
Who views with due regard each favor given,
Will prize so good a horse a boon from Heaven.
Then go, my Prince, sustained thro' life's decline,
Be ours the task to meet all wants of thine.
Enjoy the blessings Heaven in nature sends,
Rich in large pastures, shades, and streams, and friends;
Nor spoil the present good with future cares.
Contentment's a perfection instinct bears.
While man endowed with reason, hope, and soul,
On earth, must mourn his absence from the goal!

C. L. R.

Ludlow Station.
May 1, 1817.

TO —— ——.

CINCINNATI, May 5, 1817.

MY DEAR DAUGHTER :—

* * It is remarkable that the most desirable qualification with the religious and the worldly is similarly designated. The Christian faith refining our souls with the religion that is from above, pure, radiant, and easy to be entreated, full of mercy and good works, is *grace*. Easy address, and a certain dignity united with gentleness, is also termed *grace*.

I hope, my dear, you may be led to admire and appreciate rightly the graces of the *spirit*. Remember that this is the pure gold. The grace which is of the world is but a mere gilding, and, sometimes, covers the basest compound. The Lord has placed us here, and demands an improvement of our time. He has given us various talents and requires us to increase each gift. In order to do this, we must adorn the heart and mind by improving each opportunity.

* * We generally either overrate, or too lightly esteem, common occurrences; and certainly too little improve them. Unfortunately on a retrospective view, we must exclaim, Vanity, all is vanity! * * When the conceptions and emotions are placed under the superintendence of religion, they are reduced to that order which is so necessary to happy social intercourse. Without such superintendence, they degenerate to instability of character. * * *

You are about returning to your western home, my dear child. Take leave, therefore, of your friends in time, and with firmness; neither assuming the indifference of the inconsiderate, nor the sickly sensibility of the weak.

* * * * *

Your mother,

C. L. R.

The names of some of the cotemporaries of Mrs. Riske are here recorded. Others are lost to us; and were it not for these letters, retained as personal mementoes, we would know still less than we do of the praiseworthy efforts of the noble women who gave enduring vitality to the cause of religion and charity in the valley of the Ohio.

But three of her earliest associates now survive her—Mrs. General Taylor, of Newport, Ky.; and Mrs. Judge Burnet and Mrs. General Gano, of Cincinnati. At the advanced age of about eighty years, they still live to bless their families and their friends. They were among the settlers of Cincinnati when it was an inconsiderable village, environed by a wilderness. Their husbands were the leading men of the country, and their wives became closely united in the bonds of friendship. It would be difficult to find in any community, three ladies who through a long life have been more useful and more respected. They have set a beautiful example to the rising generation in all the virtues which impart a charm to home, and in works of piety and benevolence.

Mrs. Judge Burnet.
Mrs. Gen. Taylor, of Newport.
Mrs. Gen. Gano.
Mrs. Dr. Selmon.
Mrs. Dr. Allison.
Mrs. H. Kinney.
Mrs. Heighway.
Mrs. Gordon.
Mrs. Gen. Lytle.
Mrs. Gen. Harrison.
Mrs. Dennison.
Mrs. E. Symmes.
Mrs. Gen. Mansfield.
Mrs. Gen. Findlay.
Mrs. Col. Strong.
Mrs. Judge Goforth.
Mrs. Gov. Byrd.
Mrs. Mercer.
Mrs. Macfarland.
Mrs. Morris, of Columbia.
Mrs. N. Longworth.
Mrs. J. H. Piatt.
Miss Amelia Furguson.
Mrs. Lucy Este.
Mrs. John R. Mills.
Mrs. Bectle.
Mrs. Dunseth.
Mrs. Tunis.
Mrs. E. Hall.
Mrs. Col. Davis.
Mrs. Yeatman.
Mrs. Baum.
Mrs. J. F. Keys.
Mrs. E. Bailey.

Mrs. Wallace.
Mrs. Gordon, of Newport.
Mrs. Armstrong, of Columbia.
Mrs. O. M. Spencer.
Mrs. Ethan Stone.
Mrs. Prince.
Mrs. Vance.
Mrs. St. Clair.
Mrs. Griswold.
Mrs. Jacob Wheeler.
Mrs. Benj. Mason.
Mrs. Phillip Young.
Mrs. Phillips, of Dayton.
Mrs. Crane, of Dayton.
Mrs. Steel, of Dayton.
Mrs. Gen. Schenck, of Dayton.
Miss Fanny Hale.
Mrs. Cheeseborough.
Mrs. McKnight.
Mrs. L'Hommedieu.
Mrs. Catherine Smith.
Mrs. W. C. Rogers.
Mrs. David Wade.
Miss S. Wade.
Miss M. A. Burnet.
Mrs. Burgoyne.
Mrs. Stitt.
Mrs. Ruffin.
Mrs. Mary Perry.
Mrs. Cary.
Mrs. Southgate, of Newport.
Mrs. Gov. Meigs.

TO MRS. MADISON.

Cincinnati, May 7, 1817.

Dear Madam :—

The Female Auxiliary Bible Society of Cincinnati rejoice to hear that the ladies of Washington City have formed themselves into a society for the relief of orphans. These several associations are but branches of the same luxuriant vine. No class presents claims to our sympathies equal to the *orphan poor*. Cast helpless and destitute on an unfriendly world, their passions are too often brought into exercise on most unfortunate principles, and like obstructed streams, destroy the ground they might have enriched and adorned.

A new era has commenced. Man is no longer selfishly indifferent to the happiness of his fellow, but with the social affections enlarged on the solid basis of Christian charity, studies the present and future welfare of his brethren. For the children of the destitute, Heaven is creating friends. By preserving them from destructive habits, immorality, and ignorance, you are enriching the commonwealth with a supply of virtuous citizens, rendered honorable and valuable through your attention. * * * * *

May your society be blessed and guided by the sublime philosophy of the Scripture!

By order of the Board.

C. L. Riske,

Cor. Sec.

TO ELIAS BOUDINOT, L.L.D., PRESIDENT OF THE AMERICAN BIBLE SOCIETY.

August, 1817.

Dear Sir:—

The Cincinnati Female Bible Society, with hearts warmed by grateful emotion to you, who, under Heaven, laid the foundation of the American Bible Society, claim the privilege of offering a testimony of their esteem.

We have heard of your illness, and pray that your soul may experience an elevation of feeling suitable to the moment, and from the contemplation of higher scenes, acquire strength to support it.

* * * * *

Your letter to the American Bible Society will endear you to every Christian throughout the world. God is *love*, and the religion of his Son, Jesus Christ, is *charity*. These are the principles which will finally triumph over disunion and schism, unite diversity of sentiment, and give to the church its predicted stability and independence.

With anxious expectation we turn the sacred page of prophecy, and like Moses from Pisgah, cast our eyes over the promised land. Though we of the present generation can scarcely wish to live for the real enjoyment, yet what a blessed privilege to see in prospect, the time when that river of living waters which gladdens the city of our God shall flow through every land, and Zion, rising above the clouds of sectarian systems, shall stand eminently distinguished, the joy of the whole earth.

C. L. R.,

Cor. Sec.

TO WM. HAZLITT, CORRESPONDING SECRETARY OF THE TRACT SOCIETY, PHILADELPHIA.

CINCINNATI.

DEAR SIR:—

The Tract Society of this place have received your generous donation of tracts, and direct me to express their thanks to you.

In the political world, when nations or individuals are united for the attainment of one great object, rivalship creates jealousy, and destroys by producing mutual embarrassment. But in the attainment of the glorious object for which we are united, emulation produces good-will, excites concurring effort, and annihilates every selfish feeling in the universal desire to give aid. Thus contemplating the various religious associations, our blessed Lord stands eminently confessed the promoter of every public and private excellence. That the citizens of Philadelphia may abundantly share the rewards of this resplendent harvest, is our earnest prayer, and we solicit, sir, your assistance in presenting our acknowledgments to your society for this proof of our regard.

C. L. R.,
Cor. Sec.

TO NATHANIEL WHITE.

LUDLOW STATION, Feb.

DEAR SIR:—

The unanimity and peace prevailing at present, and the general desire for information on sacred subjects, lead us to hope that the time is approaching "when all shall know the Lord." We are called to labor in the same field of usefulness. The partition walls raised by pride and unbelief are crumbling; no one exalting himself above another; all, all uniting in ascribing praise, and honor, and power to Him that sitteth upon the throne, and to the Lamb forever.

Though we rejoice with joy unspeakable, we should remember that, like those who traversed the wilderness, we are by nature imperfect and rebellious sons and daughters of Adam, and like them too, prone to murmur under the most striking display of Divine mercy. It is prophesied "*they shall be taught of God;*" and while we see Bible and missionary societies directed to this great object, and the cause of truth thus promoted, we may without danger or error be confident that the issue will be glory to God and good-will to man.

The subject of your letter had our corresponding sympathies. We feel and mourn with you the sad condition of the colored people. One evening, when your letter, and the goodness of God in the present display of Christian benevolence, were the subjects of conversation, with Dr. Kinney and myself, we resolved to make an effort for the improvement of the African race, by the commencement of Sabbath schools. Under the control of the religion of Jesus, there is a power beyond human investigation, a sensibility which enlarges the affections, suppresses every selfish motive, and rises above every obstacle.

Next morning, we met to form plans for putting our designs into execu tion. Accordingly, after prayer for the direction of Heaven, we visited the houses of the colored people. We were received kindly, and with thankfulness. They were requested to meet the following Sabbath in College Hall. About forty attended. Our wishes and intentions were explained, a portion of Scripture read, and a prayer for a blessing on our efforts closed this first interesting endeavor.

By order of the Board,

C. L. R.

Cor. Sec.

TO ELISHA EMBREE, ESQ., TENNESSEE.

CINCINNATI, Feb. 6, 1817.

MY DEAR SIR :—

On my visit to this place last Saturday afternoon, I received your very interesting letter directed to the African Association of Cincinnati. With inexpressible pleasure they received your advice and encouragement; and at their request I now present you their most cordial thanks, and their full assurance of every zealous co-operation in their power, relying on the benign support of that assistance we have hitherto received, firmly believing that it is the will of the Lord, and that He will bless with success our feeble efforts, for His own glory and the good of the people.

Our association is honored by the citizens of all classes in this place. Our funds have been increased by generous donations. Some give to the amount of five dollars with expressions of approbation, and share the labor of instruction; and this disposition increases daily.

A number of gentlemen have formed another valuable institution here, entitled the "Sabbath School Union Society." One dollar paid in advance grants a membership; and the smallest contribution is accepted. Five members can organize with the assistance of the superintendent, a "branch school" which is supplied from the common fund, and taken into the fraternal care. To obtain this privilege for our poor Africans, Mrs. Kinney and myself have subscribed to the constitution, and I have no doubt of the willingness of our sisters in the same association, to unite their exertions to its completion.

In consequence of this arrangement, four of the principal superintendents met in the north wing of the Lancaster Seminary building, corner of Fourth and Walnut Sts., and organized our school according to the Lancasterian plan. The names, ages, and residences of the pupils were recorded. Several of these were over fifty years of age, and were as diligent, humble, and teachable as the youngest. They seemed very grateful, and *our* hearts were not indifferent.

A system so perfect, simple, and wise as this, must certainly be sent by the author of every good and perfect gift to facilitate the entrance of that period when it shall be said "They are all taught of God." Never to me did they appear more interesting.

When this passive ordeal was over, and order and silence again restored, Mr. Morrison joined us, and expressed his warmest sympathy and desired all to unite in prayers for a blessing on these labors of love. The effect was solemn and sublime to see nearly one hundred of the unfortunate sons and daughters of Africa elevated to the importance and dignity of citizens, fellow-recipients of the blessings of Christian society, no longer ignorant of their own capability, lounging disregarded about the streets, neglected and despised; but convened for improvement and refinement. This was one of those precious moments that occur but seldom. I believe angels looked on with corresponding praise.

Oh! that our dear sisters of Cincinnati may be enabled to persevere in this "good work," as you emphatically call it—knowing that He who loved Martha and Mary as well as John and Lazarus, is to all His creatures the same to-day and forever, and can from these associations, bring a harvest of sheaves to fill our hearts with thankfulness and praise.

Cincinnati is favored at this time in that its poverty is not despair, nor its riches annoyance. Its temporal good seems that social convenience exactly suited to the encouragement of virtue; and though there exists diversity of opinion, there is an exercise of that charity which covereth a multitude of sins. Nor is this founded on saying, Lord! Lord! but in doing the will of Him who hath said, "Feed the hungry, clothe the naked, visit the afflicted."

We pray for that blessed period when righteousness and peace will flow down the streets like a mighty stream. My dear friend, how delusive is the human heart. Morality, though founded on the Christian philosophy, is not *all*. The religion of our Lord ascends in sublime gradation far beyond earthly things. The soul sighs after enjoyments this world cannot give, and is zealous in good works, not to feed its pride, but to enjoy privileges unknown and neglected by a false estimation of the wealth it is heir to.

Our sisters send their love to you. Present our good wishes to the brethren of the Manumission Society of Tennessee; and let us, nothing doubting, be assured of the sustaining hand of Heaven in this universal impulse of love.

Resolutions.—"In this time of general engagement of the friends of humanity and this day of solemn events, while the Christian world is engaged in uniting its influence, and contributing its substance, for the spread of the gospel of Jesus Christ; and considering with grateful feelings the exertions now making among the humane of our country in behalf of our degraded race—We, a few of the colored citizens of Cincinnati, have agreed to unite our efforts in forming a society, aiding with money this good cause.

Trusting that the Almighty Ruler will bless us with one heart and one mind in this work of mercy, and sincerely desiring to follow in simplicity and truth, the injunction of the Apostle of the Gentiles, in provoking one another to love and good works, we will co-operate in the present establishment for educating the children of *colored parents* for missionary labors, and raising a school for colored people in Cincinnati."[1]

Signed by about seventy persons, and each attached his own rude mark.

C. L. R.
Cor. Sec. pro tem.

The movements of the society for the advancement of this then despised people were the first of the kind in Ohio. Its efforts were not in vain. The influence of the Sabbath school has been widely felt; and but few know whence came the first impulse to the philanthropic enterprise.

The present social condition of the colored people of Cincinnati is most gratifying. The public schools, Sabbath schools, and churches, and the multiplied organizations for literary, benevolent, and recreative purposes, are cheering proof of the susceptibility of the African mind to progress, and lead us to hope for it a far more respectable position than it even now occupies.

[1] There is no date to this paper.

CHAPTER VIII.

TO JAMES C. LUDLOW.

LUDLOW STATION, Sept. 2, 1817.

MY DEAR SON:—

* * The loss of your society is a painful deprivation; and sometimes the yearnings of a mother's heart overcome my fortitude. But I know the same kind Providence which protected Jacob, and returned him in safety to his native land, can also protect you. I hope, my son, the precepts of virtue and religion taught you from infancy, will never be forgotten. Despise the tongue of falsehood and deceit, and never make that man your friend who profanes the holy name of God. In youth you were thoughtful and devout; and I am encouraged to hope that religion in your estimation, is a possession far more to be desired than riches, honors, and the pleasures of a perishable world. Those persons only are truly great and good who conscientiously perform their duty to their Creator, to society, and to themselves.

Oh, that I could have an assurance of your acceptance through faith in Christ Jesus! I desire to see my children rich in this, should they gain it by the sacrifice of all worldly prosperity. The Lord, I trust, will lead you to choose that better possession which cannot be taken away.

Your mother,

C. L. R.

TO THE SAME.

Oct. 9, 1817.

* * I hope, my dear son, that you are not inattentive to the scenes you pass. There is in wild forests, solitary prairie, and the deep and silent flow of unfrequented rivers, a sublimity that impresses the virtuous with involuntary devotion to Him who created all things, and convinces the observer that he possesses an immortal soul, which will survive when nature lies in ruins! Amid these scenes, the mind acquires a strength previously unknown to itself, and a consciousness that we are destined for higher enjoyments. * * * *

I thank you for your affectionate letters. While contemplating the beauties of nature, may the Lord lead you, my son, to a contemplation of himself!

Your mother,

C. L. R.

TO DR. INGLES, PRESIDENT OF THE RELIGIOUS TRACT SOCIETY OF BALTIMORE.

DEAR SIR:—

With pleasure I inform you that a tract society has commenced operations in this neighborhood, and the directors have determined on writing to you for instruction concerning the best method of procuring publications. * * * *

Our country is yet imperfectly supplied with moral and religious books; and this economical plan of diffusing knowledge will, we hope, be encouraged, by all who are desirous for the improvement of their fellow creatures. We hope the time will soon arrive when Christians will join heart and hand in giving to thousands, unperishable treasure "without money and without price."

Oh! that God would indeed bless the various associations forming in His name, and hasten the blessed period when all shall know Him.

As our little association is enrolled under the same banner as yours, let us have your prayers for its success. Pray write to us.

With esteem,

C. L. R.

Cor. Sec.

TO THE MAYOR AND TOWN COUNCIL OF CINCINNATI.

March, 1818.

GENTLEMEN:—

Impressed with a sense of respect for your merit as individuals, and for the distinguished station you occupy as magistrates and *citizens of no mean city*, we address you on a subject interesting to every well-ordered mind. While we regret that there should exist among us irreligious and vicious persons deserving punishment, and acknowledge the danger and impropriety of suffering such to have liberty to corrupt others by bad example, we at the same time believe that justice and benevolence should be the governing principles of public men, and form the basis of every public and private action.

On their first visit to the Prison, the ladies of this association found the occupants few in number. The house was comfortably warm; decency and order prevailed during their stay, and gratitude for our attention was manifested by the prisoners. This created a wish, after the alleviation of their personal wants, to awaken in those unfortunate beings, if possible, attention to concerns of superior importance. It is better to go to the house of mourning than to the house of feasting, and, however incomprehensible it may appear to the inconsiderate and unfeeling, there is in virtuous activity for the amelioration of suffering, more real happiness than in the enjoyment of even Solomon's magnificence. Succeeding visits to this habitation of wretchedness, increased our knowledge of the extent and variety of the misery within, and solicitude for its alleviation.

Listening to the tale of woe without power to comfort is painful; and complaining to the impotent is unprofitable. We have, therefore, determined to request your attention to a subject offering a field for the exercise of generosity; and we hope that municipal authority, heretofore exerted in promoting social order, and planning for the convenience and honor of our citizens, will also be exerted to remedy evils that cannot be looked upon with indifference. Amidst proofs of public munificence that distinguish Cincinnati, and give it a dignified position among the cities of the United States, the neglected situation of its prison will, to the eye of any philanthropic traveller, impart counterbalancing degradation. The prison is at present in a state of decay, and its dilapidated walls, which bear many marks of the ingenuity and perseverance of men driven to despair, are inadequate to withstand attempts at escape; so that the only alternative is the additional cruelty of loading culprits with irons. When the ladies of this association last visited it, one room of about *twenty-five feet square*, contained *twenty-two prisoners.* Debtors, housebreakers, malefactors, male and female, were crowded promiscuously together, like animals in a pen for slaughter! How can those who profess to be the followers of Jesus, suffer such things to exist? Can they expect at the last day to have the encouraging words addressed to them, "I was in prison and ye comforted me?" And can the Mayor and Council of Cincinnati permit such violation of order and decency? Into this den, hard-hearted avarice and unfeeling justice claiming the *letter of the law,* plunge even the trembling female. We conjure you by those ties dear to every manly breast, as husbands, fathers, sons—by all those tender connections you venerate and defend; and by that consciousness of accountability before Him who gave you the stewardship, to unite your energies on this subject; and may Heaven give you unanimity and zeal and individual peace, is the prayer of this association!

By order of the Board,

C. L. R.

Cor. Sec.

JOURNAL.—June 14. This luxuriant farm from early care, once reached a high grade of perfection. A few years more, without the renovating hand of art, it will decline. The orchard now presented to my view, with its mingled shade and sunshine, exhibits the charms of a pictured grove. I well remember when it was planted. Rapid has been its progress. The ground, now covered with fruit-trees, was the encampment of General Wayne's army. The lines were extended from the spring in the orchard, to the spring at our door. Two rows of tents were parallel all this distance. Then the whole country was a forest. * *

Sunday morning. July.—A large camp-meeting has been held the past week three miles from Cincinnati. A immense crowd of persons was congregated. It was attended by many able preachers, warmly engaged in the conversion of sinners.

I love those dear Methodist brothers and sisters. There is among them a liberty, Christian affection, and richness of gospel enthusiasm not yet attained by us. Gracious Saviour, hasten that glorious period when Thy followers shall be one in Thee!

* * * * *

Rain has prevented our attending church. But the presence of the Lord is not limited to public assemblies. In searching the Scriptures and private prayer, our time can be profitably employed. Precious day! Oh! that we could rightly estimate the privilege of having one-seventh of our time secluded from the busy world.

* * * * *

I yet recollect a Sabbath evening walk at Loudoun. The day had passed in retirement, useful reading and conversation, when our mother proposed a walk to the woodlands. Bellá and I accompanied her. We pursued a path through the meadow around a gentle hill, and crossing the stile, came to the forest. Here we paused. On the opposite side of the meadow was a broad creek, undisturbed, as on other days, by the wheels of different mills, and reflecting on its clear, smooth surface the enchanting luxuriance of its banks. All nature seemed to enjoy its Sabbath; all was still! The distant houses in view were closed, the cattle grazed undisturbed; and Mount Parnel's summit received the brilliant rays of the declining sun. Our dear mother, aware of the importance of early religious impressions, said to us, "How sublime will be an eternal Sabbath!" * * We left the stile, when a few paces excluded the landscape from our view.

In beholding works of art, we admire the ingenuity and power of man, and the relative perfection of ourselves! From nature we receive an irresistible impression of the wisdom, goodness, and majesty of God, whose fiat created the heavens and the earth, and whose hand is equally displayed in the towering mountain, the deep valley, the lofty cypress, and the moss which spreads a mantle over the slippery rock!

The stillness of the air, the grandeur of the trees, the notes of the evening bird, with the conversation of our mother, occasioned an unusual seriousness. She spoke of the evil propensities of the heart, the necessity of virtuous principles, the importance of revelation as an infallible guide, assuring us that no mere personal advantage could secure our happiness. "It is," said she, "the religion of Jesus alone that can give peace and eternal felicity." Then kneeling, with one of us on each side of her, she prayed. I look upon this as the most sublime moment of my life. I felt myself introduced to God!

Oh, you mothers who are solicitous for the welfare of your children, before you usher them into untried scenes, as you would wish to secure to them the approbation of the good, and the protection of Heaven, lead them to God! * * * * * * * I shall never forget her! And now, in her declining years, I will comfort her in every situation, and lead her thoughts to the inexhaustible treasures of the gospel, and try to repay, in some measure, her early care in fruits of that love she so faithfully cultivated in us.

Sep. 19.—Dr. Mason, of New York, passed the day with us, on his return from Kentucky. He has a commanding presence and unusual affability. His conversation, without any apparent effort, became sentimentally pious. Such unbounded confidences, veneration, and love for Jesus, such fervent devotion, we seldom find equalled. May that God he so faithfully serves, so dearly loves, and uniformly honors, guide him through life, sustain him in death, and distinguish him in Heaven!

* * * * *

Oct. 2.—Day is dawning. Mr. Riske has passed a restless night, and I have sat by him until this moment. He has been much engaged in prayer, and at his request I read aloud in the New Testament, until finding him composed, by the advice of the physician, I have left him for an hour. How solemn is this nightly vigil! Heavenly Father, prepare me with perfect acquiescence to receive Thy decree. Strengthen me to resign into Thy hands and commit to Thy disposal, all the vicissitudes of my life.

* * * * *

TO SARAH BELLA LUDLOW.

LUDLOW STATION, Oct. 1818.

MY DEAR DAUGHTER:—

* * A few years ago, I saw the husband of my youth breathe his last, and now the husband of my age is lifeless.

* * * * *

What an awful thing is death, and how dangerous to delay preparation for it! How can a person capable of conceiving the sublimity of eternity, and the necessity of truth and holiness to make us acceptable, wait for a bed of pain to contemplate the solemn subject! when the wounding thought that we have disregarded the mercies of God and squandered opportunities, makes it doubly painful. Conscious of deserved rejection, every action—and to the awakened soul all is guilt—is brought to remembrance. Then, oh then, how dreadful the hour of darkness! But Jesus can even *then* soothe the troubled waters. To the lost sheep was Christ sent. The despairing soul finds peace in believing. This is the baptism of the spirit. This is being born again, without which an ocean would be useless could we descend to its deepest caverns.

* * I pray the Lord will pour upon you the water of *regeneration*. May that Saviour who died upon the cross, and who hath made the path plain and illustrious, lead you through the labyrinth in safety, and endow you with an inheritance incorruptible and eternal!

Your mother,

C. L. R.

Jan. 29, 1819.

JOURNAL.—A few days since, I visited the good John R. The cancer in his cheek is making dreadful havoc. But the soul immortal is beyond the reach of all the maladies of earth. I remained an hour, and during that time he three times kneeled in prayer, with such zeal for the promulgation of the gospel and success of Bible and missionary associations, that I rejoiced in the power of God, and prayed with him.

"Some people," said he, "while they see me in this extreme suffering, wonder that I am always in a praying frame. But, bless the Lord, I pray without ceasing. Keep near the Lord, my dear Christian sister, and the Lord will keep near you. Don't be afraid; Jesus is a faithful friend."

* * On the subject of inscriptions, I differ with those who in the first emotion of grief would letter the tombstone with lamentation and eulogy. We should reflect that while the cotemporaries of those who have died are living, panegyric does not rescue virtues from forgetfulness. History records the actions of the great; those who lie undistinguished by heroic exploit, are not endeared to posterity by the language of a monument. The name and some local circumstance to identify the individual are sufficient. * * But I consider it a sacred obligation to secure from violation, the grave where the human body is deposited. Yet a little while, and we shall all require the same attention.

Some days since, I suggested to a few friends the importance of a missionary society in Cincinnati. The idea was approved, and we meet to-morrow for the purpose of forming a constitution and for prayer.

O Lord! grant that there may be sacrifices and offerings, and that zeal and unanimity in the labor may not be wanting! May we as a band of sisters, faithfully enter into its duties with full confidence, trusting in Thy help.

When in 1797 I arrived in Cincinnati, it consisted of little more than a garrison of soldiers, with a few scattered houses and muddy streets. The majority of its few inhabitants wasted life in indolence and dissipation. How changed the scene! Now the streets of the busy city are crowded; hills are levelled; valleys are raised; and crooked ways made straight. Deep mire is succeeded by adamant and brick, and cabins give place to great houses; while industry, temperance, and benevolence, create for it a high respectability. The rushing steamboat has supplied the place of the slow-moving flat, and the noble Ohio river bears its commerce on the way to the ports of distant nations. * *

I like to retrace incidents which were probably the origin of my rules of conduct. * * * *

I recollect the feeling which determined my purpose, when quite young, to exercise active charity. I was spending a day with an aunt, when a poor woman, who was about moving to some other state, called to say farewell.

After her account of the expense and difficulty of the journey, my aunt opened a drawer, and gave her a large roll of linen, and the woman took her departure. I arose to accompany her to the front door, with the secret desire of giving her a dollar which I had received from my mother. There my courage failed ; I was afraid of wounding her feelings ; but I did not in the least relinquish my intention, and supposed the gate would be the better place. I took the dollar in my hand and opened the gate, intending as she shook hands with me, to leave it with her, and immediately to run back to the house. But absorbed in her own reflections, she passed without speaking, through the gate, as I held it open. I stood lamenting my want of energy. I felt as though I had erred in the sight of Heaven ; and as I had no real use for money, Providence had placed that dollar in my possession for the purpose of relieving that woman ; and I had suffered a diffidence, originating in weakness, to defeat the Divine will. This impression is not yet obliterated, and throughout my life it has been a stimulus to active benevolence.

Some days since, I received a periodical entitled "The Emancipator." I believe events are nigh which will result in glory to God, and felicity to man. Every yoke shall be broken, and oppression brought to a close.

Women are exempt from participating in legislative assemblies ; but their private influence is great. And this, modestly and feelingly exerted, would be irresistible in producing the desired effect. Pressing their children to their hearts, they might imagine the anguish of those wretched females, whose offspring are slaves from birth, whose fondest caresses are mingled with bitter sorrow; who know not the hour when a ruthless hand will separate them from their little darlings forever. * * * *

Mrs. Hannah Kinney passed the day with me. She is a valuable citizen. She unites in her character, piety, candor, and Christian zeal. Few indeed are her equal in these respects, and none more wholly devoted to the cause of suffering humanity. * *

Pain is not without its use. It conveys a lesson of wisdom not easily eradicated. In such moments, the pleasures of this world, its applause and its distinctions, are nothing. Heavenly Father! strengthen me to bear my present affliction with meekness and fortitude. * *

Many of my companions in juvenile gayety and in more mature years, are gone to the realities of a future state. The idea of an introduction into an as yet unseen world, should make religion a subject of great importance to us. It is the most valuable ingredient in my cup. Who would not possess that love which casteth out fear? How happy to know that we are under the care of a beneficent and forbearing Creator, "who forgiveth all our sins, who healeth our wounds, and crowneth our days with loving kindness!"

Night.—Almighty Father! Thou art a never-failing refuge for the distressed. My soul flies to Thee as the wounded hart to the sheltered stream. Thou hast heard my supplications, and hast not left me comfortless. Thou hast changed my mourning into praise, and I have found in Thy word an anchor both sure and steadfast. To Thy care I consign my children; keep them by Thy power through faith unto salvation. Oh! that *one* may walk with them through the hottest furnace wherein they may be cast. Only be Thou near. * *

The society known by the name of "Dorcas," met at our house to-day. This society commenced in the year 1816, with a few benevolent ladies and gentlemen. Among the latter was John H. Piatt, who has continued to contribute to its treasury annually, the sum of two hundred dollars. Others have added to its funds; and although many oppose it, it holds on its way. In March, 1818, the Board of Managers appointed a committee, consisting of Mrs. McKnight, Mrs. Catharine Smith, Mrs. Kinney, and myself, to visit the jail in order to ascertain the temporal and spiritual condition of the unhappy persons confined therein. The committee voluntarily contributed their own funds to meet all pecuniary calls incident to the appointment. The jailer, whose politeness and humanity merit our thanks, acknowledged the happy effects of these visits. The prisoners, from quarrelling, rioting, and gambling, became orderly, read the Scriptures, and frequently expressed their sense of our kindness.

Several ladies, clergymen, and physicians, assisted us. May He who numbered among His followers a "beloved physician," hail their entrance into the regions of endless bliss, with "I was sick, and ye visited me!"

* * * * *

The spirit of the gospel is one of active benevolence. The votary of Mammon shuts every avenue of intercourse with the God whose nature is love; while the follower of Jesus enjoys a feast in the blest affinity with Him "whose mercy is over all His works." * * *

Surely no tear in all the dark domain of sorrow is more precious to Heaven than the one which flows in commiseration for others, nor any act so acceptable as that which relieves from misery.

TO MRS. H., (VERSAILLES, KY.).

CINCINNATI, Jan. 30, 1819.

DEAR MADAM:—

The Bible Society of this place have directed me to address you on the subject of forming a Bible society in your town.

One of the blessed peculiarities of the Christian religion is, that no nation or sect is designated as favorite, but that all who fear God are accepted. And while our hearts are susceptible to the philanthropy of Jesus, let us under His divine inspiration, improve our time while it is called to-day, and unite our influence and resources in extending the light of His gospel.

Let us, dear sister, consider the Bible and missionary cause, the cause of perishing humanity, and esteem ourselves fortunate in having the power to aid a work so glorious. Let the selfish and the vain affect to despise it as unworthy their attention, but may Christian women never harden their hearts to the calls of benevolence.

Arise, dear sister of Versailles, and let your light shine, that others, emulous of your example, may devote their talents and means to this noble object. Consult with your neighbors ; appoint a day for meeting, and be not discouraged. That the Lord may grant you firmness and perseverance, is the prayer of this society.

C. L. R.
Cor. Sec.

TO DR. OWEN, SECRETARY OF THE BRITISH AND FOREIGN BIBLE SOCIETY.

Dear Sir :—

I am directed by the Cincinnati Female Bible Society to express sentiments of high esteem and grateful respect for the British and Foreign Bible Society.

The grand phenomenon our Lord has given, as an emblem of his approval, engages universal attention. Long may our brethren of England continue the agents of His glory! You are in the view of nations the visible acting power from which the distant machinery of the Bible and missionary societies receives impulse. He alone who directs, could harmonize such multiplicity of action. We may repeat the hallowed strain of Isaiah, "*Sing of Heaven, and be joyful, O Earth! the Lord is comforting His people.*"

In history, we find that civil and religious liberty were only prized as they opened the way to worldly aggrandizement and selfish enjoyment. Christians, rising superior to the influence of such motives, *now* seek the supreme good, and extend their hands to all; saying, with the purity and ardor of truth, "*Thou art my mother, and sister, and brother.*"

That those in the land of our fathers were the first to set this light upon the hill, is an idea pleasing to American Christians.

C. L. R.

TO MRS. ———.

CINCINNATI, 1819.

DEAR MADAM :—

In this happy land of freedom and equality, women partake with men the blessings of our national institutions; and independence of thought in religion is guaranteed as a sacred privilege. Let us act as their importance demand, and be zealous in promoting what it is our glory and honor to profess and obey.

The dreary path of female history before the light of gospel truth dawned upon the world, should impress us with boundless love to Him who has elevated us from a state of degradation. The humiliating condition of woman in Mohammedan and idolatrous countries, should excite us to emulate the fortitude and self-denial held forth in sacred pages, and to lend our energies to the great object of ameliorating our condition. It is but a few months since our missionary society became organized. Under Heaven, the idea of this association was first suggested by your circular letter. The knowledge of this fact we hope will stimulate you to further exertion.

May extravagance in dress, and all other frivolous diversion from the true purpose of wealth or character, under your auspices be reformed, and American women be aroused to consider themselves helpers in the great work of civilizing and evangelizing the world. With prayers for your success and happiness.

By order of the Board,

C. L. R.,

Cor. Sec. C. M. S.

TO MRS. PHILLIPS, OF DAYTON.

CINCINNATI, 1819.

DEAR MADAM :—

The members of the Female Bible Society of Cincinnati have directed me to address you. Increasing financial embarrassment operates seriously on the funds of this society; and judging by their own the situation of others, they consider it their duty to send word of encouragement, and to also hope that while obeying the dictates of the Holy Spirit, they may share the blessing of being comforted.

We daily hear complaints from those engaged in affairs of the world. But as Christians and moralists, let us acknowledge the Divine superintendence and direction of that Being by whom nations are controlled, and rest assured that His kingdom will be sustained amid the powers of darkness and the conflicting interests of men. We hope you will not permit these things to depress you, but with exceeding zeal exert your best energies.

One cause exists for humiliation and anxiety. Some of the professed followers of Jesus, refusing to obey the injunction, Do good and communicate, for with such sacrifices God is pleased, indulge themselves in all imaginable frivolities. If the members of every religious association would voluntarily relinquish vain pleasures, and augment their contributions in proportion, then might their light shine.

That your efforts may continue with joyful increase, is the prayer of this society.

With esteem and affection for you individually, I am, dear madam, yours,

C. L. R.,
Cor. Sec.

TO MRS. B., LOUISVILLE, KY.

Jan. 30, 1819.

DEAR MADAM :—

Hoping that the formation of a Bible society in your city will find an advocate in every one, the board of managers of this society has directed me to address the ladies of Louisville on a subject which is unfolding new and interesting progression.

With delight would we hail you fellow laborers in this cause, to assist in producing the predicted felicity and splendor of the church. Those objects are surely worthy the sacrifice of every worldly desire. Our blessed Lord while on earth honored with His friendship the daughters of Zion. Jesus loved Martha and Mary as well as Lazarus, and His religion, wherever it extends, elevates woman from degradation and misery.

If women would rightly estimate the privilege they possess in the opportunity of doing good, and make the exertion of which they are capable, and relinquish the gratification of pride of apparel, many might be brought from the regions of darkness. * * * * * Tell us of *your* unanimity, and exhort *us* to persevere as we have begun. Tell us of the sacrifices of the young, the enterprise of the aged, the prayers of the pious, and the respect of the careless. In short, tell us that Louisville has enlisted under the banner of Jesus. And that He may enrich you with treasures that neither moth nor rust can corrupt, is the sincere prayer of this society.

C. L. R.,
Cor. Sec.

TO ELIAS BOUDINOT, LL.D., PRESIDENT OF THE AMERICAN BIBLE SOCIETY.

February 1, 1819.

DEAR SIR:—

My eyes and heart were gladdened with a sight long desired, a specimen of the translation of the Scriptures into the language of our western neighbors; and from the impulse of congenial feeling, I send you congratulations. I rejoice with you; with you I raise my soul in adoration to Him who claims "*the heathen for an inheritance, and the uttermost parts of the earth for His possession.*"

Emigrating early to the West, I formed an acquaintance with many Indians, several of whom I respected as men of understanding; and I have often heard them lament the distressing situation and ungovernable passions of their people, and the avarice of the white men.

About the year 1800, in the month of June, near the middle of the day, as I sat in my parlor at Ludlow Station, commanding a view of the smooth green yard, slightly shaded from the fervor of the sun by the depending boughs of three luxuriant weeping willows, which a few years had brought to sentimental perfection—with feelings in perfect accordance with the harmony of the scene, I experienced a tranquillity of mind to which I had been for some time a stranger, and forgot for the moment that there was in all the world a human being less happy than myself.

I was interrupted by the entrance of two strangers of uncommon interest. The first was my old friend, the Delaware chief, Bok-on-ja-ha-lus.

I rose to meet him with a cordial welcome. After taking my hand, he said, "La-nah-pa-kwa (a name given me by the Delaware Indians) this is my friend Kin-ka-box-kie." They took their seats, and informed me that they had called for the purpose of taking dinner, having made the engagement with my husband in town. They were on their return from seeing the Great Father, as they called the President.

At dinner they received my attentions as persons of good breeding in those circles where good breeding excludes every useless ceremony.

Kin-ka-box-kie was taciturn. When he spoke, it was in the Delaware tongue. He desired his friend to tell me that he could not speak English. Bok-on-ja-ha-lus informed me that the President had said "they must improve their lands; their young men must learn to plough; their young women must learn to spin." He seemed dejected, but he was noble in his deportment. While we sat conversing at the table after the cloth was removed, he said, "Lah-na-pa-kwa, we now go." "And when shall I see you again, Bok-on-ja-ha-lus?" said I. "Me old; me soon lay down," said he, with a horizontal motion of his hand. Then raising his eyes to Heaven, with an ardent emotion, he added with an effusion of feeling I have never seen more expressive, "But we shall meet with Jesus." I took his hand, inquiring with rapture, "Bok-on-ja-ha-lus, do you know Jesus?" He answered with firmness, "Me know Jesus; me love Jesus." Then rising from the table, they shook hands with me, solemnly saying farewell. My eyes followed their venerable figures until the door closed from my view for the last time in this world Bok-on-ja-ha-lus and his friend.

This interview, so truly sublime, excited a more profound interest for a nation of strangers than any common circumstance could have produced, and brought to heart, with a delightful conviction of its truth, that in Christ, there is neither *barbarian*, *Scythian*, *bond nor free*.

Often have I reverted to this scene; often have I wished to contribute my mite to forward some favorable prospect of their religious improvement. And now, my dear sir, that my faith may not be dead without works, I commit unto your hands, as the friend of humanity, one hundred dollars for the department particularly of the *Delaware Translation*.

With sentiments of respect,

I am, dear sir,

LA-NAH-PA-KWA.

Journal.—During my late visit to Hamilton, the Associate Reformed Church held a protracted meeting, during which time the Lord's Supper was administered. * * * *

Precious to my soul is this feast of love. I retired with thanks to the kind hand which had led my weary steps to green pastures and cooling streams, and in the maze of the wilderness was still sustaining and spreading comforts around me.

The tranquillizing sermon, the occasion for which we were convened, the hospitality of the family who welcomed me, their pastor, the elders and their wives and daughters, and the pervading general unity—all combined to recall the days of primitive purity.

I am continually admonished of approaching death. How rapid the lapse of the last twelve months! How varied the incidents! * * How many persons lately in the bloom of health, surrounded by wealth and honors, are now in the silent tomb! That community with which they were so importantly connected that hardly a Sabbath could be spared for the soul's repose, now scarcely misses them. How many competitors in honor, rivals in ambition and power, have lost their rancor in the grave! And, alas, how soon will those who tread the same ground sink into the same oblivion, and the breasts now agitated by envy, hatred, and pride, forever cease their tumultuous emotions! Let such visit a bed of sickness, and ask themselves when thus brought low, where are the consolations to be derived from worldly pursuits?

Oh, Almighty Father, in Thy mercy lead me and mine in that humble path marked by the distinguishing graces of Thy spirit—that spirit which shone resplendent in Him who was meek and lowly, who blessed when reviled—who forgave when persecuted.

Sabbath.—Accompanied by my four youngest children, I went to church. * * * Often has sorrow been my companion to its sacred precincts. Happy is it that this refuge is open to the miserable. Here, when sinking under the burden of earthly perplexities, the heart is turned from the vanity of this life to that better one, whose wealth and honors are enduring. Here the sons and daughters of toil feel rewarded for the deprivations of the week. Here the thoughtless and the profane, from authority not to be despised, receive the plain words of admonition. Here the stranger is assured of continued protection from on high, and the desolate orphan finds a home and is comforted. And here, O Lord, I thank Thee that in Thy house the *widow*, in the dreary blank of blighted affection, in all the swelling anguish of her bosom, can find Thee unceasingly.

Should we be permitted in eternity to distinguish our friends, and also be conscious of our own identity, we will experience peculiar delight in the recognition of those whose society here constituted much of our happiness. * * * I think this will be the case. But death may, in superior wisdom, dissolve those ties so absolutely, that those born of the spirit will be united in a different and far better relationship.

The frequent recurrence of the number forty throughout the Scriptures is worthy of remark, and if correctly understood might afford a clue to the mysteries of prophecy. Forty days and forty nights rain was upon the earth at the time of the deluge. Moses was forty years old when he fled from the court of Pharaoh. Forty years after, the Lord on Mount Horeb commissioned him to return to Egypt. Forty days were the spies examining the land of Canaan. Forty days was Moses on Sinai when the Tables were written. Forty years were the Israelites in the wilderness. Forty years was the Temple in building. Elijah, the prophet of the Lord, fasted forty days when he travelled to Mount Horeb, and like Moses, on the same mountain, witnessed a display of the presence and power of God.

The destruction of Nineveh was limited to forty days. Forty days was our Lord on the Mount, and forty days after his resurrection, he ascended to Heaven. Almighty Ruler! bless the Bible associations with forty years of uninterrupted triumph to the pulling down of every imagination that exalteth itself above Thee.

Sabbath morning. * * The first church bell! Its simple harmonies unite with the affections of the heart, with the duties and solemnities of the day, and with the triumphs of the Cross of Christ.

How would its deep tones awaken the attention of the wandering Osage Indian! The sound of such a bell suspended in the fork of a great oak on the bluff of the Arkansas, would echo from hill to hill, from dale to rock, to grove and stream, prolonging the reverberation until the utmost glen would receive the invitation to the Sabbath assembly! "Clothed and in their right mind," those poor children of the forest would find, in the blessings of the gospel, cause to join in hallelujahs to the Lamb!

TO JAMES C. LUDLOW.

CINCINNATI, March 10, 1820.

MY DEAR SON:—

In the solitude of trackless forests, in the crowded city, in the tented field, and in all the grades of civilization, man is everywhere the same complex, mysterious, and inconsistent being, fluctuating from one extreme to the other; the sport of accident, the slave of habit, the machine of prejudice, and the child of folly; with blind infatuation engaged in pursuits injurious to others and ruinous to himself. He acts correctly, rather as the result of surrounding circumstances than of established rules of conduct. A selfishness indulged from infancy, contracts the circle of his usefulness, and extends only as other objects offer superior attraction. How important then to the future prosperity of such beings, to inculcate virtuous principles in early life.

* * I lately met with a narrative of one well educated and respectable, and who had lived after the manner of the irreligious, until he was laid on the bed of death.

His eyes were opened to the unprofitableness of his life; and becoming greatly alarmed at the prospect of death, sent for a pious friend to converse with him. His friend spoke of the merciful dealings of God to the rebellious children of Israel in the wilderness, and to David and Manasseh. "Alas!" said the dying man, "there may be promises and consolation in the Bible for such a sinner as I am, but I have never read it." Oh, how lamentable! Ignorant of the character of God, ignorant of himself, without time to seek knowledge, what was there to prevent his soul from sinking into eternal ruin? * * *

My dear child, I hope you will remember my numerous injunctions, and search the Scriptures while in health. They are able to make you wise unto salvation.

In answer to your inquiries with regard to the various denominations of Christians, we lament the diversity of sentiment, but confidently hope that unanimity will prevail. At the same time, it is natural and proper when we are instructing our children in religious knowledge, that we should teach them our own faith. We teach them our language, dress, and manners, and why not our religion? Your father delayed attaching himself to a church; but he was a firm believer, and united with me in the sacred ceremony of baptism when you in infancy became a member of the visible church. And now, my dear child, search the Scriptures, and after attentive investigation, choose for yourself. I resign you to the merciful protection of that Saviour to whom you were dedicated, trusting that we shall meet again at the right hand of God.

Your mother,

C. L. R.

TO SARAH BELLA LUDLOW.

July 15, 1820.

My dear Daughter:—

The perusal of a well-written book is a luxury I should be unwilling to relinquish. But plays and novels, in my opinion, generally convey false estimates of principles and men; create a morbid sensibility; inculcate unjust ideas of propriety; present improper standards of duty, and unreasonable views of life. I have always endeavored to guard you against this seductive and unprofitable waste of time, by forming a taste for natural history, philosophy, and belles lettres. Such studies will increase your knowledge, and afford material for reflection and conversation in proportion to the amount of reading. Ideas thus acquired, will do you honor when produced.

Amidst all your engagements, my dear child, neglect not the daily study of the Word of God, with an application of its solemn truths to your own soul. * * * The Scriptures teach us that life is but a transitory existence, a state of discipline and trial, and our chief pursuit on earth should be to prepare for a more intellectual and happy state of being beyond the grave.

Your mother,

C. L. R.

TO JAMES C. LUDLOW.

CINCINNATI, August 2, 1820.

MY DEAR SON:—

After acquiring property in houses and lands, we should account ourselves criminal in neglecting to have our estate *made sure*, lest some misfortune should occasion the loss of all. Our *rights* here are the possession of a day, of a moment; while the rich inheritance of Heaven is eternal. This we neglect to secure, and hazard its loss forever, by our procrastination and folly. Those blessed with the hope of a happy future, pass through life unruffled by the vicissitudes of fortune, and use their best endeavors in pressing forward to the mark of the prize of the high calling.

In answer to your request to visit Missouri, I have concluded, my dear son, to make you a visit of a few months. But so uncertain are all human calculations, and so changeable the state of my health, that I must form all my plans, and make the necessary arrangements in case of my death. The Lord will direct. * * *

The depressed state of money matters creates much uneasiness among our business men. The gentlemen have formed an association for the reduction of family expenses, superfluities of dress, amusements, &c. Mr. S. insisted upon the entire disuse of tea and coffee. Dr. Drake argued against the measure. He said that tea and coffee prevented intemperance by supplying our laboring classes most happy hours, and that it was also too great an enjoyment of refined society to be relinquished without danger of a resort to some substitute more expensive and more injurious. In his opinion, there would be one hundred drunkards to one now, were they dispensed with. * * *

Your mother,

C. L. R.

Journal. * * Memory often reverts with pleasure to a visit made about twenty years since, to the residence of Dr. Morrell. After tea the first evening, I looked around, and observing but two beds in the room where we sat, was apprehensive that we might occasion some inconvenience to the family. When evening worship was concluded, the Doctor took a lamp, saying to us, "You have been travelling, and would like to retire early. Pray accompany me, and I will conduct you to your room."

The moon had risen full, and was shedding its light on the neat white-washed fence inclosing the yard. The night was calm, and the atmosphere delightfully cool. From a rustic piazza, we stepped on a straight "puncheon" walk, at the end of which, surrounded by shade trees through which the moon was glimmering, we saw a neat, low cabin. In the front were one window and a door, with a few hewed log steps laid before the latter. The Doctor opened the door for us to enter. Delighted and surprised, we there found a clear blazing fire, a smooth white hearth, a case filled with choice books, a table, chairs, carpet, etc. "Here," said he, "is your own apartment; consider this as your home. Be as much with us as you can; but when you choose to retire, here are books, and water, and shade, and undisturbed hours." There was something in it so romantic and so perfectly charming, that we took our seats and dwelt on every detail of the artless incident.

* * * * *

My old friend, Capt. Seron, called on me this evening. He has always been esteemed a man of integrity. The first time I saw him after Mr. Ludlow's decease, was at a large camp-meeting at Springfield. He pressed through the crowd, and taking my hand, told me to look to Heaven for comfort in all my trouble. "My dear Christian sister," said he, "my heart participates in your sorrow. The woods of Turtle Creek can witness the ardor of my prayers in your behalf!" There are moments when the heart's emotions are so exquisite, that its chords vibrate to passing influences, like the harp of Æolus. Responsively they were touched by the pathos of the figured "woods of Turtle Creek!" The solitude so dear to me, awakened by sympathy a thousand tender images.

Capt. Seron has since then joined the Shakers, and though I cannot see with them that their faith is the truth, yet I have too high an opinion of him, to suppose him a hypocrite. The uniformity of his character while "in the world" ought to secure him from that charge. It must be an error of judgment.

I once sat by the bed of a neighbor, who was almost expiring. She pressed my hand and said, "I look forward with joy to my dissolution; my days have been days of sorrow; a union which death alone can dissolve, has embittered my existence; and I rejoice that freedom from the *yoke* is the consequence of dying! I will soon be in that place of rest, to which I have been long a stranger. Oh, what a mercy!" she exclaimed with uplifted hands and eyes, "in Heaven there is neither marriage, nor giving in marriage."

* * Before daylight this morning we were awakened by the plaintive notes of a bugle. The melody sank and swelled, languished and revived, again and again, awakening the soft responses of retreating night, and lulling all around to silent attention. Associating with the sound the mournful recollections of long since fled happiness, my heart rose and fell with its varied symphonies.

Well may the imagination add to the joys of Heaven, the ecstatic charm of music. Perplexed with harassing cares, how soothing, when every note is in sentimental accordance. When in praise to the Almighty, the soul finds expression in strains of rapture holy and sublime! * * * * *

* * * * *

CHAPTER IX.

SEPTEMBER 1.—Accompanied by my dear friend Mrs. McFarland, and my two little daughters, I yesterday made a farewell visit to Ludlow Station. The ride was peculiarly agreeable to me, after many weeks' confinement to the dusty streets of a city. After repose, we rambled over the woodland. Softly murmuring flowed the beloved stream of Mill Creek. Precious to my view are its verdure-clad banks. Often with the husband of my youth have I climbed the hills around; often, seated in the cool shade, has he narrated the dangers of early times, while yet the savage footprints were fresh in the sand.

*   *   *   *   *

*   *   *   *   *

When Mrs. Riske first went to the farm, she devoted her spare moments to the judicious disposition of vines and shrubbery of familiar sight and fragrance; and thus kept afresh the sweet memories of the home beyond the mountains, which filial love and youthful association had dictated as the model of her own new place.

Years have come and gone since Ludlow Station was presided over by the subject of this sketch. It bears few traces of its former beauty; and all there is left to remind us of the tasteful hand that imparted cultured grace to the lavishness of nature, are two willow-trees. These were planted by Charlotte Chambers. They are old and rugged now, and are swiftly hastening to inevitable decay. Under one the railway stretches its iron track, and the rush of the rolling train will disturb its flexile boughs for two or three seasons more. When this old willow-tree and its weeping mate are level with the earth, hideous in their mangled deformity, the last vestige of Ludlow Station, and of her who subdued its rougher features, will have passed into unending oblivion.

The recollections of him who perilled his life in the far west and lost it when so young—the agony of the widow bereft of a protector and plunged in the cares of children feeble in years—the management of a large, unproductive estate, and the many harrowing trials that beset every woman in a similar situation, afford aught else than a happy picture.

Sometimes we, who live in Clifton, walk along the brow of the hill that slopes to the valley beneath, and take in at a glance the Station farm. The declining summer sun brightly floods the yellow grain fields spread out before us in great checkers amid green meadows, and casts long shadows from the groves and isolated trees scattered over them. In the grass inclosures, herds of motley-colored cattle quietly grazing in kaleidoscopic group, or winding in drawling file toward the barns, harmonize with this placid scene. In the distant cemetery, on the open sward and among the maples, we can see the pure white headstones marking the graves, and the tall monuments crowning the hillocks. On the broad avenue leading to the narrow ways that follow the inequalities of the swelling ground, an ominous line of dark carriages, preceded by the sullenly repulsive hearse, moves in slow procession. From the belfry at the gate, a solemn knell vibrates with lengthened pauses through the still afternoon, and creates in us a strangely wild and dreary feeling.

In another direction nearer to us, from the village the confused hum of factories, the sharp clear-ringing clink of the blacksmith's anvil, and the clatter of a light wagon on the dusty road, reach us in poetic measures. In the hazy illusive glow, the forlorn aspect of the old house, half environed by a wilderness of spontaneous locust and ailantus trees, and the giant willows overshadowing all, combine to make us pensive in viewing these changes of sixty years. Ah! the charm of Ludlow Station has departed forever, and we must seek in the homes of those who are yet spared to us, the concentred solace which can nowhere else exist.

Not long after her mother's decease, Mrs. Riske was confined to her bed by an asthmatic affection. Extreme physical debility ensued. All the available medical remedies failing to benefit her, a change of climate was proposed in the hope of relief. She considered her sickness an infliction of Providence for some wise purpose, and cheerfully bore her sufferings.

Many reasons influenced her to prefer a western tour. Her eldest son and other relatives were living in Missouri, and she felt that her efforts for Christianity would meet with more abundant return in those regions where the harvest was plenteous and the laborers few.

Her friends in Cincinnati, fearing that the fatigues of the trip would exceed her powers to resist them, and that she might expire on the way, opposed this selection. Her response was, "'As the day is, so shall thy strength be.' If the Lord has work for me, he will enable me to do it; and relying on His promise for support, I will go in His name."

Accompanied by her youngest son and her daughters Ruhamah and Charlotte, she commenced the long and tedious journey across the States of Ohio, Indiana and Illinois, and through Missouri, almost to its frontier border.

The difficulties accompanying her progress would have been unendurable but for a heart so imbued with a desire to serve the Lord, that no useless repinings escaped her lips. All she saw were sources of rapture. Her soul was filled with Divine reverence, and poured forth a continual anthem of praise. She frequently caused the carriage to stop; and in the midst of the lonely group, kneeling on the grassy roadside, would lift her voice in prayer to the Great Architect whose monuments were the eternal hills, and whose handiwork showed forth on all sides in unbroken majesty.

In this spirit she travelled. Sometimes on leaving the house which had sheltered her for the night, a Bible or tract remained—often where its teachings were before unknown; and religious advice and prayer were affectionately offered, when fitting opportunity presented.

TO MRS. HEIGHWAY.

CINCINNATI, Sep. 8, 1820.

DEAR MRS. HEIGHWAY :—

Two years have passed since I parted with you. Many painful circumstances have transpired, but mercy has predominated. The great truth is daily impressed on me with increasing importance—that in this life is not our home.

My health still declining, we have determined on a visit to Missouri. I anticipate with exquisite pleasure, leaving heated rooms, crowded, bustling streets and dust, for a journey through woodland shade and flowery prairie. I shall often reflect on the many happy hours enjoyed in Ohio. But should the number of my days be finished before arriving at my destination, I shall have the same power to support me that could alone be efficacious here.

We have lately received information from the Osage Mission. Two of the young ladies, Miss Hoyt and Miss Lyon, are dead. Miss Hoyt once visited me, when I was very sick. I said to her, "venturing on a field of such deprivation and trial, endears you to my heart." She answered, "Oh! who knowing the value of their own souls can hear and disregard such a call?" On taking leave of me, she held my hand a moment and said, "I shall see you no more in this world; but we will meet at the right hand of God." Then turning to one who was in attendance, "I hope, my dear young woman, you possess the one thing needful." There was such dignity, zeal, and love in her manner, that I viewed her with admiration. She has gone to receive her reward. The moment of her death was better than the day of her birth. I congratulate her on her joyful entrance into the regions of immortality.

* * * * *

Farewell,

C. L. R.

TO MRS. GANO.

CINCINNATI, Sep. 16, 1820.

MY DEAR MRS. GANO:—

Circumstances having occurred to prevent my crossing the river, I shall therefore reluctantly be obliged to relinquish the pleasure of seeing you before I leave this country.

It is a solemn occasion when we bid farewell to those we love—to those who have soothed our sorrows. I believe I can better sustain the trial of parting with the whole group than with them individually, and particularly with one whose uniform gentleness and affection have made her so dear to me as you. May the Almighty bless and comfort you in life, be with you in death, bless your children with the influence of His Spirit, and finally grant that we may meet in the mansions of rest prepared for those who love His name. Tell General Gano that a thousand associations unite his image with one yet dear to my memory.

I am preparing to leave this town with more fortitude than I expected. To me the scenery on the journey will present charms congenial to my feelings. Heaven has blessed me with peace and resignation surprising to myself. How infinite are his mercies!

* * * * *

Farewell. Be assured, my dear friend, the remembrance of your love will help to gild the cares of

C. L. R.

September 18, 1820.

JOURNAL.—My kind physicians, Drs. Ramsey and Pearson, recommending a journey, after making it the subject of prayer, I took my departure from Cincinnati for Missouri, accompanied by my youngest son, my two little daughters, a woman servant, and a careful man to drive the carriage. I experienced many regrets when bidding adieu to a place so attractive to me by innumerable and delightful reminiscence. My protracted indisposition, and still doubtful prospect of recovery, give a solemnity to the parting, connecting with it the idea of final.

* * * * *

Leaving the precincts of the city, I turned to take a last look. Love and admiration for it forced from my heart the exclamation, "How goodly are thy tents, O Israel!" Oh, Cincinnati! may the God of Jacob enlarge thy borders, preserve thee from tumult and every evil, and increase thy love and zeal in His service! The regrets awakened by the incidents of the morning were banished by reflecting on the gratitude due to Sovereign goodness.

* * * * *

As we progressed, the beautiful Ohio was on our left, its banks ornamented by native forest, through the luxuriant foliage of which the glittering beams of the sun gave a tremulous lustre to the slow moving waters. A serious impression on the minds of our little party obliged me to reanimate by cheerful observation their almost exhausted spirits. Reflection I did not dare indulge in. I well knew my own heart, which can more easily prevent the feelings arising from tearful recollections, than suppress them when excited. * * *

Just at dark we arrived at the hospitable mansion of General Harrison. Himself was there to welcome us, and his well-known voice at once dispelled our remaining sadness. * * * *

TO SARAH BELLA LUDLOW.

North Bend, Sep. 19, 1820.

My dear Daughter :—

I hope you did not long indulge the emotion awakened by our separation. Do not, my dear child, give way to painful apprehension on my account. You know the same God is with us on our journey who preserved us from accident at home. Then trust in Him. Let us glorify God. Events, with their causes, are under His control, and His everlasting arms support us in all places, and under every circumstance.

When I survey the mercy our Heavenly Father has ever manifested, and find by experience the influence of His grace in subduing wayward passions and affections, and bringing all into captivity to the Cross, I bless, and wonder, and praise. I can commit my children, myself, and my cares to His superintendence, assured that He directs. But though unseen, let that power be adored and sought. Live near to God. Keep your mind in a habitual sense of his presence. Be cheerful—be true. Suffer not the levity of the moment to lead you into hyperbole of expression, so much the fashion with the thoughtless, and which renders their actions and their words a falsehood. Speak truth so that a mathematical reasoner listening to your most unguarded expression, would attach an adequate idea to every word, and find them important, innocent, and necessary.

Your mother,

C. L. R.

JOURNAL.—The next morning we left North Bend. The road became more hilly as we progressed, and the country presented a bleak aspect. Owing to the steep hills and the unimproved state of the roads, the whole party, except myself, pursued the way on foot.

After a fatiguing day, we came to a number of new buildings, and requested accommodation for the night, which was granted. The family were natives of Scotland, and from their manners and language, I supposed they had once the advantage of better society than those desolate hills afford.

At the town at Madison, we left the Ohio river, and pursued a more directly western course. In ascending a very high hill, we beguiled the fatigue by anticipating a delightful prospect on arriving at the summit. But the intervening trees and thick underwood obscured the towns and farms our imaginations had pictured. How just an emblem of the busy worldling! He labors to acquire an eminence his heart delights to contemplate at a distance, as the summit of all that is desirable on earth; but after attaining it, he finds himself as far from happiness as in the valley from whence he emerged, and as circumscribed in his affections and powers.

Sunday, Sept. 24.—At White river, we stopped to rest the horses, and refresh ourselves. We loitered on the banks of the beautiful stream, admiring its quiet and picturesque loveliness. The water flows in an equal current over its bed of rock, so perfectly level, that it maintains an equal depth from one shore to the other, and the banks are smooth, green, mossy and romantic. The place where we sat, commanded a view of the mill, the bridge below it, the falls, and the pellucid stream reflecting its banks. But the inhabitants of this beautiful spot were silent and dejected; almost the whole of them lying sick. The town was in gloom, with the doors and windows closed, or only opened to exhibit the inward wretchedness. The mill was silent; no busy wheel in motion; and though thus it should be on the first day of the week, yet we associated it with the surrounding affinities.

This stream we have just crossed is the "East fork" of White river, the "West fork" we expect to cross to-day. These lands were once in the possession of the Delaware Indians. Their principal town is situated about sixty miles distant from this place. Were it nearer, I should certainly visit it, out of respect for the friends I formerly numbered among that once powerful, but now almost extinguished, tribe.

Sept. 26.—The approach to Vincennes from the east, exhibits the town to great advantage, in a line of pleasing perspective. We were prepared to see almost a city. Objects viewed in the distance are generally estimated falsely; their faults or perfections being magnified according to the disposition of the observer. On entering the town, the narrow crooked streets, ruined fences, roofless houses, and unglazed windows, gave it the appearance of poverty and wretchedness, although a few neat modern buildings were interspersed. All seemed idle. Sickness had closed the doors, unnerved the arm of industry, and subdued the desire of display. The low state of the Wabash river and its sluggish current, is supposed to occasion, in a degree, the unhealthiness of the place.

I have often thought that the life, designated happy or unfortunate, is owing more to the medium through which we view the circumstances controlling it, than the facts themselves. Should we, ungrateful to Heaven, and ungenerous to each other, see only the imperfect and disagreeable portions of our journey, we might tell of the chilling prospect, bad roads, dull hours, and monotonous progress through the prairies; the gloomy woodland, the dilapidated cabins with rude floors and exposure to observation, the ignorance of the people, the abundance of insects, the scarcity of water, &c. But we try to acknowledge the blessings we experience. * * * *

Oh! Thou whose power sustains us in every situation; smooths the way; softens the air; suppresses the storm; gilds with brightness the darkening horizon; calms the mind, and solaces the heart! Thou ever gracious God! Continue Thy infinite goodness toward us, and strengthen our resolves to devote ourselves to Thy service.

TO MRS. HEIGHWAY.

VINCENNES, Sept. 1820.

DEAR MRS. HEIGHWAY:—

You will be surprised to see my letter dated at this place. I know your affectionate heart will beat for me.

My nervous affection spread its baneful influence over my best energies. Sorrow for the loss of a beloved mother incapacitated me for struggling with a disease which finally acquired force, until I feared it was permanently settled in my system. However, the Lord was pleased to bless the means used to allay it, and enabled me to look around with renewed interest on ties that connect me with the world.

I was three days in a situation my attendants considered dangerous, but that Power who has ever sustained me, left me not. My soul could contemplate the dissolution of its frail tenement undismayed, and resign its cares. Without His omnipotent arms beneath us, how could we support the trials of this life? Increasing experience of His forgiving love through the Lord Jesus, confirms the reality and efficacy of His religion to strengthen us. Oh! how many are tampering their hopes of immortality in Heaven, for the fleeting, delusive pleasures of earth.

Although many trials have been mingled in my cup, yet in my declining hours I have innumerable blessings. My beloved children are all believers. I am surrounded with friends, and to Him who liveth forever,

I can say *Abba*, Father. Farewell, and be assured, my dear Mrs. Heighway, of the sincere affection of your friend,

C. L. R.

Journal.—After crossing Little Wabash, distant from the Great Wabash forty-eight miles, we arrived at a well of water, so isolated and so very opportune to the weary traveller, that we thanked the unknown hand who had placed it there. Feeling its necessity, we learn to estimate the value of water. Abraham contended for his wells with the herdsmen of Abimelech. But Isaac being a man of peace, to remedy the evil, multiplied his wells. On digging the last one, he found a supply of water sufficient for the demand of all the herdsmen of Gerar and his own, and he called the well Rehoboth.

We crossed another beautiful prairie with its smooth green carpet, and picturesque clumps of trees extending far and wide. If fire was the potent agent in clearing the timber, why are those isolated groves left. Conjecture is useless. I will henceforth but admire.

> "Not deeply to discern, not much to know,
> Mankind were made to wonder and adore."

We were told that the Delaware Nation, consisting of about six hundred men, women, and children, were a few days' journey in advance of us, moving to the more western regions. They are abandoning their once ample and deeply prized domain, for which they fought and bled, and where their fathers are buried. Unhappy people! May God sustain them in their wanderings, prevent them from discontent, and their strength from failing, supply them with food, and send the gospel of love and peace to guide them into the mansions of the blest.

About nine o'clock in the morning we entered the "Grand Prairie." Rich pillar clouds, encircling the widely-extended horizon, enhanced the beauty of the prospect. With a feeling of solitude, we silently pursued our way. * * *
A little circumstance gave the finishing touch to the picture. A wolf

entered our path a short distance before us, and trotted on, smelling the ground as if following a trail, until a turn of the road and the high grass hid him from our view.

A large number of emigrants were encamped near where we passed to-day, and their sheep and cattle were scattered in all directions in quest of grass, and the woods resounded with the tinkling of bells. This recalls the days of the Patriarchs. Like those men of the olden time, these stop to be refreshed, pitch their tents under the shelter of a spreading tree, converse and recline in supreme ease, and feel as though the cares of this world and they were disunited.

Man is surely by nature inclined to a wandering life. Necessity compels him to earn his bread by the sweat of his brow, or never would his brow sweat! How mistaken are many in the estimate of happiness! Theatres and ball-rooms are little things compared to the romantic banks of "Silver Creek," or the expanse of heaven and earth in a single view on an Illinois prairie.

On crossing the Mississippi river, the change in the soil was plainly manifest. The ground was black instead of light, and the timber was of walnut, poplar, sugar-maple, ash, and locust. Vines, climbing from tree to tree, suspended great bunches of grapes. Various other fruits were there in exuberance.

The ground continued to rise until we saw the opposite bank, with which our course lay for some miles, almost parallel. Huge masses of rock composed the bluff. Solid and high, it seemed cut into finished design. I requested my children never to forget the grandeur of the figure, "The Rock of our Salvation." The same Almighty hand that sustains the universe sustains the soul! The God of nature is the God of grace. With awe and reverence for that Being who poured out the streams and spread the sky for a covering—who adorned the way with plains, and streams, and flowers, made the fertile valleys, and piled the amazing and stupendous rocks—I caused the carriage to stop, and said to my little family, "Here, a note of praise to the All-wise Creator, the incomprehensible Jehovah, has never yet been heard. Let this be so no longer. I will exert my weak voice, and the banks and lofty trees will echo back the sound!" We all kneeled, while I raised my voice in prayerful adoration to God!

We stayed one night on a solitary prairie. The distance across it was ten miles, and night came without a house in view. Much of the way was "prairie wood." A new road had escaped our observation, and after progressing some distance, we were stopped by fallen timber. We, therefore, returned to the more open ground for safety should a storm arise.

It required fortitude to support a situation so desolate. The children, with the sweet pliability so amiable in infancy, and so lovely in more mature years, quietly submitted to the arrangement without indulging one fancied evil, considering the real one sufficient. They bore without a murmur the crowded position, and tried to make me comfortable by offering me all the cushions. The coachman was uneasy about the horses, as they strayed in search of pasture. He therefore, wrapped himself in his great coat and kept watch. My good maid Kitty and I sat on the back seat, muffled in our cloaks, but too anxious to sleep much. I provided for the comfort of the children, and she watched the stars to see how soon morning would come. The air was mild, and the sky unclouded. I was delighted with the splendor of the heavens. Owing to the purity of the atmosphere, the stars looked larger than I had ever before seen them. The moon displayed her crescent above the eastern horizon. Venus beamed in all her placid loveliness. Jupiter was south, the galaxy distinctly luminous, and the Ursa-Major took his nocturnal round in all the brilliancy of an autumnal night.

The last prairie on our journey is said to be twenty miles across. The horses seemed stationary, and to be treading an inclined plane without gaining the point of ascension. Conversing on the origin of prairies, I was amused with the observations of the children. One said, "She thought God had made them so at the first; that even burning them down would not prevent the sprouts from rising again, unless it was continued every year, and that the trees now around and interspersed through them are all that were ever there." "Yes, mother," said another, "you know it was as easy for God to make a prairie as to make a forest." "My dear little Christian philosopher," said I, "you have accounted for them on the most amiable principles, and henceforth I am a convert to your opinion. The Lord has displayed the infinity of His power in the variety existing in every order of creation, and I hope, my children, that you will continue to ascribe the mysteries we cannot solve, to His will, assured that such is our wisest plan."

With health improved to outward show, she reached the town of Franklin, Missouri, which was her destination on leaving home.

She immediately commenced her labors of love, and after much effort, formed a society, and received a box of Bibles from Cincinnati. She intended going to the town of Chariton, thirty miles higher up the river, for the same benevolent purpose, but untoward circumstances prevented it. The winter was unusually severe, and detained her in doors for the major portion of its wearying months. She bore this restraint with the composure and resignation of an humble follower of the Cross. Her exertions in the cause by letters and conversation were unflagging, and her prayers for its glorious success never ceased.

TO MRS. BURGOYNE.

FRANKLIN, MISSOURI, Oct. 31, 1820.

DEAR MRS. BURGOYNE:—

We arrived at this place, after a journey of nearly six hundred miles, performed in eighteen days. The weather was remarkably fine; the roads good; the children in health; and sublime and enchanting rivers, stupendous hills, unmeasured prairies, rocks and forests relieved the tedium of our solitary way. We were preserved in safety through all danger, though once we had not a house to cover us. Darkness overtook us before we reached a habitation; but we commended ourselves to the protecting care of Providence, and no evil came near.

From the low grade of general improvement in the State of Indiana, I fancied every cabin without a Bible, and had my supply afforded it, I could have entered on the important inquiry with pleasure. But the exertion of the individuals themselves, is necessary to render the gift a blessing. Salvation must be earnestly prayed for. "*Jesus, thou son of David,*" brought a blessing after the Lord had passed by.

One morning while waiting for breakfast, I conversed with the landlady. She mentioned the destitute state of her neighborhood, and said, "Were it not for occasional visits of travelling preachers, the Word of God would be almost unknown." She had been educated to the faith of the Associate Reformed Church, with all its sectarian prejudices, but she could now say, "Blessed be he who cometh in the name of the Lord,"—Baptists, Methodists, Presbyterians, all were welcome who could preach Christ. A neighbor entered the room, and was listening with much attention to the conversation. She said that she was lately awakened by the preaching of one of those travellers. Her husband was a deist, and she was without a Bible. I sent to the carriage for one, and presented it to her saying, "the Lord has seen your tears with compassion, and has sent you a Bible." Her eyes filled, and drops in quick succession rolled down her cheeks. "If you have another Bible," said the good landlady, "I must ask it for another neighbor who is in the same condition, with the additional charge of a family to rear and educate." I granted the request of this worthy woman. How easily could a few such form a Bible society! The Lord would send abundance for the supply of the needy around them. There is a false delicacy, a diffidence which sometimes prevents the exertion necessary for success, even in the cause of truth. * * *

May the grace of God be with you,

C. L. R.

JOURNAL.—On the tenth of November, we made an excursion to the mouth of the Lamine river. We crossed the Missouri with some difficulty, the wind being high. This river is always muddy, swift, and deep, and does not overflow its banks. From mistake of early travellers, it was considered a tributary to the Mississippi, when it is the principal stream.

Mr. —— was assiduous in securing us a safe conveyance across the river. With much surprise I found him to be an avowed disciple of Thomas Paine. I find many here openly despising all religious societies and the sacred observance of the Sabbath. It is my paramount wish to see a Bible society established in this barren country, and to labor to my utmost for its advancement. O Lord, arouse my energies, and give me strength even for one week's labor! Thy power is almighty! Give me that faith in Thy efficacy which can remove mountains. * *

Jan. 1, 1821.—This day twelve months ago, my beloved mother was taken ill, and in two weeks from that time breathed her last. Since that period, my health, then delicate, has been daily declining. A late paper from Cincinnati mentions the decease of Mrs. Ziegler. My heart pays a tribute to her merit. Faithful, candid, and kind, I ever found her, and life has lost another charm which gilded its sorrows with a smile of love! Dear and valuable Lucy Zeigler, my heart bids thee a short farewell! Almighty Lord and Saviour, I commit my soul and feeble frame to Thee! How rich are the prospects of Thy mansions of everlasting rest!

* * * * *

My sweet children, soon will these tearful eyes weep no more, and this palpitating heart of her whose constant care has been your welfare, cease to beat. To God I commit you. He alone is able to save.

* * * * *

TO ——— ———.

FRANKLIN, MISSOURI, March, 1821.

MY DEAR MARY :—

We have received the account of your little babe's death, and shed a tear to his memory. Alas, tears will not bring him to view again! But I hope God will allay your grief and soothe you to peace. The Lord gave him to you for a short time, and He has taken him away. While the feelings of nature incite us to murmur, Grace should teach us to submit. *Shall not the Judge of all the earth do right?*

I know your native gentleness; but, my beloved Mary, mere passive resignation is not enough. Faith in the promises will carry us out of self, and make us acquiesce from a sense of superintending wisdom. Jesus will secure the everlasting inheritance of your babe in those mansions prepared for His people. To His protection let us resign our children and our own souls. Our bodies shall rest in their graves until the resurrection. Glorious hope!

Why some live to old age, and others are snatched away in the prime of their most useful days, is mysterious to us. It is the will of God. Let not your heart be troubled. Not a sparrow falleth to the ground without our Father's knowledge, and the very hairs of our head are all numbered. Jesus explained why the Jews could have no power over his life in the extremity of their malignity. My time is not yet come. In all of Job's trials, *he sinned not, nor charged God foolishly.* Let us also submit to the Divine will, and manifest the truth of that religion which teaches us, that with the Almighty there is no *chance*, no contingency in the widely extended sphere of His government. The sorrowing sisters of Lazarus imagined that had Jesus been there, their brother had not died, and they thought, as we too often think, that prudence and forecast might have preserved life. But Jesus was not ignorant of the events passing in the house of Martha.

* * * * *

With sincere affection,

C. L. R.

JOURNAL.—A Bible society is at length formed in this "dry and sterile land." I thank Thee, Heavenly Father, for this ingredient in my cup of mercies. I thank Thee for this refreshing of my soul. Lead and direct this infant institution, and guard it from the malice of the enemies of Thy cause. Increase the number of its friends, and their zeal in this good work, and enrich their souls with a perfect knowledge of those truths and consolations they have engaged to distribute. May they go on to perfection until Thy Word shall have a clear course, and until the light of the Gospel shall shine throughout this region of darkness, and to Thy name be all the glory. Holy, holy Lord God Almighty! exert thine omnipotent power, and reign king of nations as Thou art king of saints!

* * * * *

March 14, 1821.—How kindly the Lord is dealing with me! Again I am able to venture in the open air. How delightful after a winter's confinement is the vivifying warmth of a calm opening spring! O Lord, sanctify this to my recovery, if it is Thy will. Nevertheless, not my will, but Thine be done!

April 10.—I have been very weak and much indisposed these ten days past, but greatly sustained in pain of mind. How infinite, O Lord, are my obligations to Thee! I stand on a rock which can never be shaken. * * * * *

I have a new cause for thankfulness, arising from a call to labor in the vineyard. A circular addressed to me at Cincinnati was forwarded to this place from the missionary society of New York. It contained an address to the Christian and the benevolent community at large. Agents were chosen throughout the several States to act in unison with the society. Mine was the only female named in that whole catalogue.

* * * * *

O Lord, unworthy—unworthy am I of this Thy notice. I am far distant from Cincinnati. But with Thy aid, I may be enabled to reach it in time to unite my influence and labors with the beloved sisters of that place. * * * * *

Thou art a strong tower! My soul rests in Thee, and finds safety. The weakness of my heart and the imperfections of my character are forgiven in the immensity of Thy love. My soul, although as crimson, can be made white as snow. * * I am low, but Thou art high. I am weakness, but Thou art power. Sustained by Thee, I am enabled to rise above earthly cares, and calm and resigned await Thy will. * * * * *

Vain are all my fears, and fruitless my anxieties, only as they lead my mind to Thee. I can only seek such comfort from Thee, my Saviour, Thou dear physician of my soul and my body. To Thy sovereign will I bow, and in full conviction that it is well, I rest. * * *

Sanctify the fervent aspirations of my soul. From Thee they emanate; in Thee they centre; and whether many or few be the days of my pilgrimage, let my best energies be spent in Thy service—for Thou knowest that my most glorious hopes and my most precious treasure are established in Thee. * * * *

I thank Thee, gracious God, that Thou art comforting me. In all my sorrows, Thou art leading me to Thyself. To Thee I commit this desirable object. Oh, carry it on to perfection, and hasten the time when Thy watchmen shall see eye to eye!—when Thy sheep shall be one flock—when righteousness and peace shall encompass the earth, and infidelity, ashamed, will hide its guilty head. * * *

* * * * *

Evening.—O Lord! I thank Thee for the sweet tranquillity of this day. Unworthy as we are, Thou art still unchangeable. Thou art my light, my shield, and my hope. Weary and heavy laden, my soul will find its rest in Thee. And wilt Thou, Almighty Father, listen to one so unworthy as I? Yes, I know Thou wilt, and I shall continue to trust in Thee. Oh! sustain me and protect my children, who are soon to be left without my guardianship. I consign them to Thee!

April 30, 1821.—The air is still chilly, and the roads bad, but I wish to commence the return journey.

Should my days draw to a close on the way, sweetly would I, surrounded by my little family on the shaded banks of a purling stream, bid farewell to earthly cares. How much more delightful thus to die, than in close rooms with air deprived of its vital principle, to one panting, suffocating, dying! Oh! be Thou then present, my God, and all will be well.

* * * * *

May no marble rise in stately magnificence over my dust; but let me rest under the soft, flowing turf, where, amid the waving of the long prairie grass, the ever-sighing winds can breathe a requiem to my spirit!

* * * * *

* * * * *

* * * * *

Not long before her death, two young missionaries were in Franklin, on the way to a distant Indian station. At their last visit to her, they knelt by the bedside and made their parting prayers with great fervor and devotion.

When they ceased, she arose from her recumbent position, and requested them again to kneel. The friends and relatives present also knelt; while she, laying her hands on their heads, poured forth in thrilling tones, an invocation to God for the abiding of His Holy Spirit in the minds of those youthful disciples, and to make them powerful in winning souls in acceptable obedience to Him.

The stout hearts of the young men were deeply affected. In the rapture of the moment they freely gave way to tears of joy and love. Not a dry eye was in the room, as they solemnly departed from the presence of the sainted one who had offered to the Throne of Grace the glowing symphonies of inspiration.

With perfect submission to the supreme command, and entire knowledge of her approaching dissolution, she calmly dictated her will; adjusted other secular matters, and expressed herself ready to go.

On the twentieth day of May, the hour came. She had no fear; and even when she felt the icy hand of Death, its presence was so gentle, and its progress so gradual, that she would inquire, "Is this death? Oh! let me die triumphantly."

She looked tenderly at her sister, and with a smile of celestial love said, "Grieve not for me, my dear sister. I will be the first to welcome you to Heaven."

Supported by pillows, she asked for all of the household, and took leave of them, addressing each with appropriate words of consolation and encouragement. After this, her whole being was absorbed in the prospect of the glory that awaited her. The last words she uttered were, "Oh! let me lay my head on Jesus. Come, Lord Jesus! Come quickly!"

FINIS.

www.ingramcontent.com/pod-product-compliance
Lightning Source LLC
LaVergne TN
LVHW011209110826
845150LV00006B/1380

* 9 7 8 1 4 2 5 5 1 7 6 5 6 *